# LOOKING FOR LOVE IN ALL THE RIGHT PLACES

by
**Richard Gosse**

Published by
R & E PUBLISHERS
P. O. Box 2008
Saratoga, California 95070


Library of Congress Card Catalog Number
84-60394


I.S.B.N.
0-88247-735-8

*Dedicated to Matt McKay*

# TABLE OF CONTENTS

# THE DESPERATELY LONELY

Imagine you are desperately hungry. When you're starving, you don't insist on a gourmet meal. You'll settle for scraps. So, too, with the desperately lonely. They get involved with the first available person. They're always in a relationship, no matter how painful, because for them the greatest misery is being alone. The desperately lonely have no need for this book. They have no problem meeting someone for a romantic relationship, since just about anyone will do.

The people who need this book are those who are selective, those who prefer being alone to being involved with the wrong person. While there may be 60 million singles to choose from in America, it's difficult to find that special person who is right for you.

Meeting someone special requires hard work. Don't listen to people who tell you the opposite. They believe in myths. For example:

1.  The Enchanted Evening Myth. The song from the musical *South Pacific* says it all. One night your life partner will be across a crowded room and it will be love at first sight. This actually does happen—for about 1% of the population. 99% of us are not so lucky.

2.  The Zen Myth. This says that when you look for somebody you will never find them. Only when you give up your search will the right person walk into your life.

1

This is similar to telling someone that the easiest way to get a job is to take a vacation. That's baloney.

It amazing to see the contrast between how much effort people are willing to exert for their careers and how little for a fulfilling relationship. It says a great deal about their hierarchy of values. They will do almost anything to get ahead: spend many years and thousands of dollars for the right college degree; buy the right clothes; spend unlimited hours on the phone and going to job interviews; shamelessly flatter bosses they can't stand; accept transfers to places they hate. When it comes to love, however, they shrug and say, "When the time is right, it'll happen."

Satisfying romantic relationships usually don't just happen. They take work and most of all patience. Unfortunately, choosy people sometimes don't know **how** to find the right person. They wind up moving into the desperate category because they had to wait too long.

The purpose of this book is to enable you to stay selective long enough to meet the right person. With this book, you will:

- Learn where to go to meet attractive people of the opposite sex.
- Receive step-by-step instruction on how to overcome your fear of rejection.
- Learn the art of conversation and how to be a good listener.
- Learn how to abandon your prejudices and stereotypes.
- Find out if your expectations are realistic.
- Learn how to increase your attractiveness.
- Discover your resentments toward the opposite sex and how to get rid of them.
- Learn how to cope with flaws in others.
- Be given the tools for surviving loneliness.
- Learn how to transcend the games that singles play and develop honest, intimate relationships.
- Find out how to keep love alive.

I want to level with you. There's nothing magic in this book—just skills that take hard work to learn. It's tough to meet the right person. But it can be done. Millions of people in this country are happily in love right now. You can join them.

# WHY CAN'T I FIND
# THE RIGHT PERSON?

There are millions of discouraged singles in this country. Male or female, the refrain is the same: "Where are all the single women?" "Where are all the single men?" Both sexes seem equally convinced that there is a terrible shortage of the opposite sex.

Obviously they can't both be right. The fact of the matter is that there are close to 60 million single adults (over 18) in the United States. While you are reading this there are literally millions of men and women hoping to meet someone for a loving relationship. Why, then, is it so difficult to meet the right person?

A sociological explanation currently in vogue is that we live in an impersonal, urbanized society that causes us to feel isolated from each other. In "the good old days" it was easy to meet people. Most of the population lived in small towns where everyone went to the same schools, playgrounds, churches, barn dances, etc. Even in the big cities it was easy to meet people because everyone felt part of the neighborhood. People knew and greeted each other on the street. They tended to fall in love, marry, and raise children in the same area.

Today it's rare to find a sense of neighborhood in the big cities. A study of Chicago's South Shore neighborhood revealed that residents visit friends *outside* the neighborhood more often than within the area and that almost half never visit with the neighborhood at all! The authors of the study concluded that "South Shore is in fact primarily a bedroom for its inhabitants."[1]

Social isolation is certainly a plausible answer to the question of why it's so hard to meet people, but it fails to identify what may be the chief culprit—extreme selectivity. Nathaniel Branden, in *The Psychology of Romantic Love*, points out that throughout the world romantic love is seldom the ideal—nor was it even in the United States until recent decades. People got married for economic and child-rearing purposes, not love. Divorce was an abomination. Divorcees were seen as immoral and a threat to polite society. A woman was expected to stay with her husband regardless of his personal inadequacies. Wife-beating, alcoholism and impotence were "crosses to bear". A man who traded his wife in for a younger model was looked upon with disdain and punished severely by alimony laws.

Today Americans see marriage as a means to happiness, not as an end in itself. Cognizant of the high divorce rate they are more choosy about whom they will marry. They wait for Ms. or Mr. Perfect. Few ever match up to their romantic ideal.

Part of the problem is Hollywood. Men look at the movie or television screen and see Farrah Fawcett and Jane Fonda. The result is that 95% of men seem to be chasing after 5% of women who are slim and beautiful.

If you are a woman, resist the temptation to pat yourself on the back for being less concerned with physical attractiveness than men. Own up to your own superficial expectations. Most of the women I have interviewed are prejudiced against guys who don't have a large salary and a status job. In my work with a dating club, time and again I spoke with women over the phone who said yes to a physician or lawyer who wanted to date them, but said no to a janitor or truckdriver.

Women may be less concerned about physical appearance than men, but that's not to say that it's unimportant to them. Most women want a good-looking boyfriend, much as most men want a pretty girlfriend. The sad fact, however, is that only a tiny percentage of single men and women are going to look like playboy bunnies or movie stars. In fact, even playboy bunnies and movie stars don't look that way in person. The Hunchback of Notre Dame would look good with the right make-up, clothes, hairstyle, photo retouching

5

and camera angles. The occasional "knockout" or "hunk" you see walking down the street proably has a long line of admirers. Unless you're also beautiful or have some equally desirable quality (like a million dollars), chances are you won't succeed with them.

Let's assume that you do meet your photogenic dreamboat. Everything may not come up roses, as James discovered. "I felt very fortunate when I started dating Barbara. She was every man's dream: beautiful face; long, full, jet black hair; all the right curves and long, slim legs. The first night we went to bed I thought I had died and gone to heaven!

"It took about a month for the bubble to burst. I started to notice how stuck-up she was. I've got nothing against high self-esteem, but this was different. She had the attitude that the world owed her a living. Everyone had to kowtow to her because she was so beautiful. I guess I really don't have a right to complain. After all, Barbara didn't change—I did. I got tired of being her humble admirer. I started to feel that she was using me, not just financially, but in other ways, too. Our relationship never graduated from the excitement of the chase to the joys of intimacy. They only come from an equal relationship.

"One other thing that got me was the boredom. Barbara didn't have much of a personality. She wasn't stupid—she had an above average I.Q. But she wasn't witty and she wasn't much of a conversationalist. She was a great status symbol and sex object for me but after awhile, she really wasn't all that stimulating anymore. Now I'm going with a girl who isn't half as gorgeous as Barbara, but that's okay. I guess maybe the old cliche is true about beauty only being skin deep."

Take care not to misinterpret James' experience. Beautiful people are not all stuck-up, nor are they all boring. Be aware, however, that we all have both faults as well as good qualities. Less attractive people from a physical standpoint sometimes compensate with other virtues.

**EXERCISE**

How high are your expectations? This is not an exercise about your fantasies but about what you will settle for in a romantic relationship. On a scale of 1 to 10, 1 meaning extremely attractive and 10 meaning extremely unattractive, what is the rock bottom that would satisfy you in the following areas:

_____ 1.  Looks
_____ 2.  Wealth
_____ 3.  Intelligence
_____ 4.  Sense of humor
_____ 5.  Honesty
_____ 6.  Social status
_____ 7.  Education
_____ 8.  Psychological health
_____ 9.  Maturity
_____10.  Pleasant disposition

Now measure *your* attractiveness to the opposite sex. Self-appraisal is not an easy task. Be as honest with yourself as you can. Don't put down what you wish you were like or what you'll be like "after I lose 5 pounds this month" or "when I make my fortune next year". This is an exercise on how attractive you are *today*. By the same token, if you have a tendency to be overly critical or judgmental about yourself, inflate your score a point or two to counteract your modesty. You may find it helpful to show your self-evaluation to others whom you can trust to be honest. Going to a flatterer is a waste of time. Rate yourself on a scale of 1 to 10 in terms of your attractiveness to the opposite sex.

_____ 1.  Looks
_____ 2.  Wealth
_____ 3.  Intelligence
_____ 4.  Sense of humor
_____ 5.  Honesty
_____ 6.  Social status
_____ 7.  Education
_____ 8.  Psychological health
_____ 9.  Maturity
_____10.  Pleasant disposition

## SHOULD I LOWER MY EXPECTATIONS?

Are your expectations much higher than what you have to offer? If so, you are in deep trouble. Why would anyone with the qualities you demand settle for you? If you are a 3 in looks and a 5 in wealth, you are unlikely to attract someone with a 10 in either category. On the other hand, you don't necessarily have to score high in the same categories as the person you desire. For example, it's not unreasonable for a person who is a 10 in wealth to expect someone who is a 10 in looks (or vice versa).

In many cases it is essential to lower your expectations. For example, Joe is a 36 year old divorced carpenter. He is average looking and rents a one bedroom apartment. Joe loves young, beautiful, slim women. He spends a great deal of time at home—alone. The beautiful women all seem to be taken, or at least that's what they tell him. Joe fails to realize that the women he wants are few and far between and have their choice of more wealthy and attractive men. Joe reads his *Penthouse* magazine each month and fantasizes about all the beautiful women he will have—someday.

Let's also consider Rachel, a 25 year old brunette with large brown eyes and a beautiful smile. She works for the phone company and has never been married. Rachel has one main problem: she could "afford to lose a few pounds". Occasionally she gets offers for dates from single guys at work, but she usually turns them down. She's holding out for a doctor, lawyer, or business executive. Rachel comes from a poor family. Her father was a blue collar worker who was frequently laid off. Making it financially was a struggle for the family and her mother always told her that "it's just as easy to fall in love with a rich man as a poor one."

Both Joe and Rachel live in a dream world. Joe is no more likely to marry his girlie magazine foldout than Rachel is to wed a future millionaire. They have years of loneliness ahead of them because their expectations are too high. Both would be wise to come down to earth and settle for what is reasonably available.

The other side of the coin is the classic mistake of overcompensating. After years of loneliness many single people decide "I'm just too fussy" and abandon their expectations. Susan, for example, is a 41 year old school teacher and mother of two teenagers. Long ago, when she married Phil, he was in law school and she thought she had hit the jackpot. Years later she found out that he was a homosexual and divorced him. Susan is pretty and still has her figure. Unfortunately, the professional men she dated seemed to always leave her for younger women who didn't have any children. Realizing that "I'm not getting any younger," she said yes to the first marriage proposal she received. Jack is fairly good looking, a nice guy and owns a stereo shop. There's only one problem: he's not the brainy type like Phil. Susan misses the deep philosophical discussions she shared with her first husband. Jack only likes to talk about electronics, cars and sports, all of which bore Susan. A mistake has been made, caused by overcompensating.

Charlie is a 27 year old photographer accustomed to working with physically attractive women. Not wanting to "fish off the company pier," he searched for his dates elsewhere. Charlie initially only dated beautiful women but got tired of standing in line for occasional dates with "prima donnas". He started dating Mary, who is average looking and a sweet and loving woman. Charlie kept telling himself what a wonderful woman Mary was and how lucky he was to have her. All of his friends told him he'd be a fool to let her get away. Finally, after six months, he tied the marital knot. Now that he's married, Charlie finds himself fantasizing about the models he meets at work while making love to Mary. Their lovemaking is down to once a week and mostly out of a sense of obligation. Charlie keeps thinking that he is fortunate to have Mary, but his body just isn't responding.

If your expectations are realistic, in time you will find someone right for you. Just be patient and stick to your guns. Don't make the mistake of lowering your expectations and settling for someone who won't meet your needs. Try to keep two things in mind:

1. Don't expect people to change. For some reason, men and women delude themselves into thinking that whatever shortcomings their partners have will disappear after marriage. They seldom do. Get involved with people who meet enough of your expectations to satisfy you. Don't think that love, encouragement, criticism, anger or nagging will change them. Accept people as they are or move on to someone else.

2. Trust your feelings. Don't argue with yourself and try

to convince your body or mind to be turned on to someone you think you should find attractive. Physical and emotional attraction are primarily subconscious decisions. You have little volitional control over your romantic tastes and desires. You may find yourself madly in love with someone who is almost the complete opposite of what you think is desirable. On the other hand, you may meet someone who seems to meet the basic requirements you have but feel apathetic. Your heart has "reasons" that your mind may not understand.

What do you do if your expectations are unrealistically high? There are several options:

1.  Lower your expectations. This is more easily said than done. The first step is to honestly face the fact that you probably are never going to get the kind of person you desire. Feeling the truth, rather than knowing it intellectually, will enable you to let go of your unrealistic expectations. Be patient with yourself. Give yourself time to absorb all of this. In a month or two, re-do the exercise in this chapter. Hopefully, you will find that your expectations have been lowered.

2.  Eliminate any expectations that are non-essential. What do you have to have from your future mate in order to be happy? Hal, a 55 year old dentist, put it this way: "I'm looking for a lady whom I can love and who will love me. The rest is negotiable."

3.  Increase your attractiveness to the opposite sex. This is the subject of the chapter entitled "Looking Good".

4.  Get your life working well in other areas while you're waiting for a loving relationship. If you're happily single, you won't be in a hurry. See the chapter entitled "Surviving As A Single".

5.  Be like Avis and try harder. If you put more time, energy, money, feeling and intelligence into meeting people, you will succeed where others fail. The next

chapter tells you how.

## FOOTNOTES

[1]Taub, Richard P., et al., University of Chicago. *American Journal of Sociology*, September 1977, p. 430.

# PLAYING THE NUMBERS GAME

Most singles find themselves on the horns of a dilemma: Do I wait months, even years, for the right person or do I take what I can find right now? Fortunately, there is a way to avoid both extremes. Learn how to play the Numbers Game.

The secret to winning this game is to meet a large enough number of prospects so that one of them is likely to be right for you. A prospect is someone of the opposite sex who is single, available for a loving relationship, and lives reasonably close to you.

Unfortunately, most people lose at the Numbers Game. They meet small numbers of prospects each year and wonder why they never find the right person. They end up by themselves, lonely and depressed.

Most singles could easily double or triple the number of prospects they meet each year and correspondingly double or triple their chances of finding the right person. There are three cardinal rules for successfully playing the Numbers Game. Before turning to these rules, let's first look at where many singles do meet.

Simenauer & Carroll surveyed 3000 singles for their book, *Singles: The New Americans*. They report that one-third of singles meet their romantic partners through friends. Apparently the classic blind date is still effective. As a first step towards meeting someone special, spread the word to your friends and relatives that you are looking. Hopefully they will invite you to dinners, parties, etc., where you can meet all of their single friends. Be aware, however, that most of them will not attract you if you are a selective person.

College students have the best chance of meeting a romantic partner through a friend. Professional people, who are most likely to have moved away from home or otherwise lost contact with their high school or college social set, have the least chance of being introduced to the right person.

Unfortunately, many singles hate blind dates. They feel their friends have a bizarre concept of what turns them on.

## MEETING PEOPLE AT WORK

Simenauer & Carroll report that one-tenth of singles meet their partners at work. There are many advantages to meeting people in a business setting:

1.  Meeting them is almost automatic. You don't have to be forward in order to introduce yourself to your fellow workers, superiors, clients or customers.

2.  Usually you see the same people repeatedly. The relationship has time to grow gradually. You don't have to start dating someone until after you know enough to be sure that a good relationship is possible.

3.  People are often very attractive at work because they are doing something that demonstrates their talents and abilities. You are also likely to be more attractive when you are performing a job for which you are well-suited.

4.  Usually there is a feeling of comradery and togetherness at offices or businesses that brings people together almost effortlessly.

Be aware of the hazards of meeting people at work, however. Amanda is a 27 year old stenographer. "I fell in love with a guy in the office and lived to regret it. After we broke up, there was a horrible atmosphere in the office. Half the people were on Roger's side and half on mine. You can't easily disengage yourself from someone you have to see each day. It took a long time for us to even become semi-

13

friends again."

Another problem with dating people at work is the lack of privacy. No matter how discreet you are, somebody always finds out. Then the gossip begins. Serious problems can arise if you date your boss or one of your subordinates. Cries of favoritism and petty jealousies almost invariably follow.

If you're not meeting the right person at work or through friends, it's incumbent upon you to search elsewhere. There are three simple rules to help you win the Numbers Game. If you're a typical single, the chances are that you're consistently violating one or more of them.

## RULE 1: GET OUT OF THE HOUSE

It's amazing how many people violate this rule. The only time they regularly leave the house is to go to work. That's fine if there are numerous prospects at the office but most people are not so lucky. Many singles fail to meet the right person at work, stay home almost seven nights a week, and yet can't understand why they never meet anybody special.

Women in particular are guilty of violating this rule and for good reason: they are more vulnerable than men at night. Both men and women complain about the cost of going out. And even if they have the money, they don't have the energy. It's tough to work full time, eat dinner and then go out searching for someone special.

These are all good excuses, but they won't help you find the loving relationship you want. You aren't going to meet anyone by watching television each night. Getting out of the house regularly is an indispensable first step for winning the Numbers Game.

Let's assume that inspired by this book, you're constantly out socializing. Your television becomes covered with cobwebs from lack of use and your children start calling the babysitter mommy. Does this guarantee that you will meet the right person? Unfortunately, the answer is no. Forget about Rule 1, Get Out Of The House, unless you are willing to obey the next rule. What's the use of braving the elements, paying for babysitters, subjecting yourself to the dangers of murder, rape, mugging and getting hit by a truck? All that sacrifice is a complete waste unless you succeed in meeting someone special. This is only likely to happen if you're willing to follow the next rule.

## RULE 2: GO WHERE THE DUCKS ARE

If you were a duck hunter, you wouldn't go inside a movie theater to shoot ducks. You might have to drive many miles away to an appropriate rural setting where ducks congregate. The same holds true for romance. Find out where the ducks (prospects for a loving relationship) are and go there!

Unfortunately, most singles go where the ducks aren't. For example, they visit their friends. This is great if your friends have loads of visitors who are prospects for you. But usually this isn't the case. If you want to meet prospects, you need to go where there are plenty of strangers, not friends. This goes against the grain because we are far less comfortable with strangers. Remember, though, that it is also uncomfortable to be lonely the rest of your life.

Besides the mistake of only visiting friends, the other frequent error is only going to places where there are people of your sex. Let's face it. Men usually feel most comfortable around other men and prefer to do "masculine" things. Most women likewise would rather get together "with the girls" and do "feminine" activities. There are major differences between what men and women traditionally do in their leisure time. If you don't believe that, count the number of women playing basketball in the local gym or the number of men in a sewing circle. To find out how well you are observing Rule 2, do the following exercise.

## EXERCISE

Make a list of all the places you went to in the last 30 days for social reasons. Next to each place, write an estimate of the number of ducks (single people of the opposite sex) whom you didn't know that attended the social event. If your problem is that you attended events where there were no ducks (or very few), decide to attend at least one event per week which is loaded with ducks until you meet someone special. The crucial question, of course, is where are all the ducks?

To find out the answer, ask people of the opposite sex where they "hang out" for fun. Tell your relatives, neighbors,

15

fellow employees, etc., the kind of person you want to meet and ask them to suggest some places to go searching.

## WHERE ARE ALL THE WOMEN?

When I lecture to men, I usually suggest taking an aerobics class (also known as dancercise, jazzercise, etc.). If you go to an aerobics class, you will usually find at least 10 women for every man. I hasten to add, however, that there is a catch. I took an aerobics class and was a little cocky when I walked into the room. I appeared to be in better shape than most of the members of the class. I figured that this would be a snap! I'd run circles around these women. Twenty-five minutes later my muscles started to cramp up—muscles I never even knew I had. Five minutes after that the pain became severe. Now it was a matter of pride for me. I wasn't going to say uncle when I could see "out-of-shape" women persevering. Five minutes later I collapsed in an agony of muscular spasms. I finally discovered why some say that women are the stronger sex. So men, beware.

Another place loaded with ducks is folk dancing: Greek, Israeli, Balkan style. Women often love folk dancing; most men don't. Todd is a 45 year old attorney. "I used to want to be part of the disco crowd but never had the nerve. There were too many guys to compete against. Besides, I couldn't stand the ear-shattering music. One night, I went out folk dancing and was shocked by the contrast. There were three women for every man! The music was beautiful and the noise level was just right. A shy guy like me had no trouble finding someone to dance with because all the dances were in long lines. Over a year I dated women from the folk dancing almost exclusively. Eventually I wound up being in a committed relationship with Gloria. Now we still go out folk dancing, but as a couple."

## WHERE ARE ALL THE MEN?

If you're a woman looking for prospects, you don't want to take an aerobics class or go folk dancing. Where do you go? One obvious place is a singles bar which usually has a surplus of men. Another activity is sports. While most men love sports, most women are not interested in athletic competition. You can have all those healthy hunks for yourself.

I mentioned basketball before. If you went to the local

gym some evening, you probably would be the only woman there. Unless you're over five foot seven, though, you might get trampled. Perhaps a more realistic suggestion is volleyball. I started a singles volleyball club a few years ago. Everybody had a great time but we had one problem— a perennial shortage of women. Maybe they were all afraid of breaking their nails.

Sue is a 19 year old student. "Antonia, my best friend, asked me to join her softball team. She said it was a great way to meet guys. I told her she was nuts. I've always been incompetent at sports. In grammar school, I was always the last girl chosen on a team. The only way Antonia got me down to the first practice session was by promising me that I could drop out immediately if I wanted. I found out that I wasn't as clumsy as I was in school. I even got a base hit! I was really afraid of fielding because I wasn't very good at catching or throwing the ball. The team captain said, "no sweat". He assigned me to the outfield where nobody ever seems to hit the ball anyway. Now, thanks to softball, I've got a fun activity each week, lots of new friends, and a steady boyfriend."

Tennis was once a great suggestion for meeting men. Thanks to Billie Jean King, though, there are almost as many women as there are men on the courts today. Golf is much better. It's still primarily a male sport.

One additional advantage to all sports, including racquet ball, touch football, and many others, is that they are marvelous exercise. You will find that keeping your body attractive is easier if you play sports.

## CLASSES

Call your local college, high school, or recreation department and ask for a catalog of adult education classes. There are likely to be dozens of choices, some of which should appeal to you. Many of them will be loaded with ducks. If you're clever, you'll ask the adult ed coordinator for advice. Which class has the most women? Which has the most men?

Mary, a 33 year old legal secretary, always had a thing for guys who looked like Arnold Schwarznegger. She took a weightlifting class at the local college. Her girlfriends couldn't stop laughing. They thought she had lost her marbles. They aren't laughing anymore. Mary is going steady with a guy who makes Hercules look like a runt.

Roger is a 41 year old cable television installer. "I originally took cooking classes because I love to cook. An unexpected bonus was all the single women who hit on me. I didn't have to lift a finger to meet them. I later found out that some of the guys in the class couldn't care less about learning how to cook. They just wanted to meet women."

## CLUBS AND ORGANIZATIONS

There are countless clubs and organizations that are ideal for meeting people. Find out which ones have the most prospects and join. Irv is a 34 year old factory worker. "I've always been interested in politics so I decided to campaign for Republican candidates. Unfortunately, all the women at the campaign meetings were either married or unattractive. I decided to check out the Democrats. After all, everyone knows that whoever wins an election is probably going to do a lousy job anyway. The Democratic women were a little liberal for me, but who cares? They were single— and nice. Now I meet all kinds of women at victory parties and campaigning door-to door."

Joining a political party isn't the only way to be politically active. There are a lot of action and pressure groups. You can join one that pushes rent control, ecology, better public transit, nuclear arms control, cutting taxes, or fighting crime. The possibilities are endless.

If you are apolitical, there are numerous other options. Turn to the yellow pages of your telephone book and look under Clubs. As an example, here are the listings in the San Francisco Directory:

| | |
|---|---|
| Bridge | Engineers |
| Motorcycle | Epicureans |
| Outdoors | Travel |
| Backgammon | Senior Citizens |
| Boats | Jazz |
| Professional Women | Old Timers |
| Tennis | Rod & Gun |
| Chinese-American | Athletic |
| Musical | Philippines |
| Political | Polish |
| Public Affairs | Press |

Diners Out                    Puerto Rican
Eagles                        Rotary
Elks                          Russian Center
Bowling                       Teamsters
Commercial                    Marines
Garden                        Smooth Dancers
German American               Golf
Yacht                         Italian
Outdoors                      Optimists
Indoor Sports                 Police
Irish                         Soroptimists
Islamic                       Sports Car
Benevolent Association        Stock Exchange
Jesters                       Conservation
Kiwanis                       Neighborhood
Alumni                        Transportation
Lawyers                       Vintners
Lions                         World Trade

If these clubs don't provide enough choices, the Yellow Pages suggest that you also look under the following headings:

Associations
Athletic Organizations
Business & Trade Organizations
Chambers of Commerce
Consumer Protection Organizations
Fraternal Organizations
Fraternities & Sororities
Health Maintenance Organizations
Human Services Organizations
Labor Organizations
Political Organizations
Professional Organizations
Religious Organizations
Senior Citizens Service Organizations
Social Service & Welfare Organizations
Veterans & Military
Women's Organizations
Youth Organizations & Centers

Surely one or more of the multitude of clubs and organizations listed in the telephone book might appeal to you.

You may consider volunteering to work for one. By so doing you will be performing a public service and meeting many new people. Mariel is a 48 year old divorcee. "I called my local Volunteer Bureau and wound up doing office work once a week for the Heart Association. I really got off on helping with a good cause, but the main thing was that I got to meet a few attractive guys. I'm still dating one of them on a semi-steady basis."

As in the case of adult education classes, don't waste your time with clubs and organizations that don't have any prospects (unless the other rewards make them worthwhile to you). Some organizations have more ducks than others. Join them.

### HUMAN POTENTIAL GROUPS

Since the sixties, large numbers of Americans have flocked to encounter groups, awareness workshops, discussions, weekend retreats, etc. An extremely high percentage of the people that attend these human potential groups are single. Also, people who participate in these activities have a tendency to be more sincere and open than average. Since the emphasis in these groups is to provide a warm, supportive environment for people to take risks, the prospects for intimacy are higher than in almost any other kind of social interaction.

Jerry is a 39 year old plumber. "I always shied away from encounter groups because I figured everyone there would be all screwed up. A buddy of mine suggested I sit in on his group one night. I found out that the members didn't have any more (or any less) hangups than anyone else. The big difference was that everyone there was fairly open. A lot of the normal game-playing was missing. I got involved in a great relationship because I first got to know her gradually in the group.

### MEETING PEOPLE AT HOME

Although usually staying home doesn't work, sometimes your home can be the perfect place to meet people. It has the advantage of being a place where you feel comfortable and safe. If you throw frequent parties, coffee klatches, lunches, brunches and dinners, you may very well meet an attractive person without stepping out the door. Also consider organizing recitals, performances, lectures, discussion groups, etc. in your home. You can make your home the party and recreation center for the entire community!

Tim is a 38 year old paraplegic. "Going outside in a wheelchair each night can be a drag. It's a lot easier if people come to me. I organized a bridge club that meets free at my home each week. We have lots of fun and I get to meet new people occasionally."

## PARTIES

How do you throw a successful singles party? First, it's vital to invite people you don't know well along with your close friends. Otherwise it's highly unlikely that you'll make a new contact. One way to do this is to hold a "pyramid" party where each of your invited guests is asked to invite five additional people.

You may be reluctant to throw a party for any of a number of reasons. One may be cost. Certainly a party can be expensive if you hire a caterer, cook a lavish meal, or serve drinks. But a party need not be costly to be successful. Here are three ways to keep your expenses to a minimum.

1. Ask your guest to "bring your own bottle" (BYOB). This is quite common, particularly if most of the guests are going to be strangers. You provide the cups and ice; they provide the booze or soft drinks.

2. Throw a Potluck Party. Assign your guests specific types of food to bring. You can do this on an individual basis (Charlie brings the apple streudel, Mary brings the wine, Alma cooks the pork chops, etc.), or by last name (A - L bring the salad; M - R bring a main dish; S - Z bring the dessert).

3. Provide inexpensive food (e.g., potato chips & dip, cheese & crackers, celery & carrot sticks). You are usually not expected to provide a meal to guests at an evening party.

Your pride may not allow you to follow the above suggestions ("I don't want anyone to think I'm chintzy."). If that's the case, it may be better to go to the expense of hiring a caterer than to cook the meal yourself. If you're busy all night cooking and serving food (and cleaning up afterwards), you won't have time to enjoy yourself. Worse yet, you won't get a chance to connect with anyone, which is really the purpose of the party.

One thing you may want to do is select a theme. There are all kinds of good reasons or excuses for throwing a party. For example:

1.   Housewarming parties, if you've just moved.
2.   Birthday parties for yourself and friends.
3.   Holiday parties, such as Christmas, New Years, Valentine's, etc.
4.   Seasonal parties, such as end of the summer, springtime, etc.
5.   Final divorce decree parties.
6.   Astrology parties (each month is an opportunity to celebrate a different sign of the zodiac).

## WHAT ABOUT YOUR NEIGHBORS?

Have you considered the possibility that someone special may be living in the apartment upstairs or the house down the street? How well do you know your neighbors? It's amazing how many of us don't even know the names of the people next door. Here are several suggestions for tapping what may prove to be an excellent source of romantic prospects.

1.   Keep an eye out for new people moving into your apartment complex or street. Offer to help carry a few things into the house or to loan them lightbulbs, coffee, sugar, etc. Do this even if they're married or of your sex. They may later introduce you to their attractive single friends or relatives.

2.   Introduce yourself to all of your neighbors if you haven't already. You can do this casually the next time you see them or make a point of knocking on all the doors of neighbors you don't know and saying hello.

3.   Invite your neighbors over for a cup of coffee or glass

of wine and say yes when they ask you to enter their homes.

You are particularly fortunate (or shrewd) if you live in a large apartment complex populated predominantly by singles. Frequently these complexes have swimming pools, recreation rooms, saunas, hot tubs, and tennis courts, which are ideal for meeting people. Don't be a stranger; become a part of the social life of your complex. Be on the lookout for parties at the recreation room or neighbors' apartments and make sure you get invited. If no one else is willing, take the initiative and organize a "meet your neighbors party."

## PICK-UPS

Are you aware of the thousands of singles you pass by each year just in the course of your daily life? Supermarkets, banks, laundromats, elevators, beaches, parks and even sidewalks can be excellent places to meet people. Making contact with a stranger under these circumstances is usually called a "pick-up". Surprisingly large numbers of singles use this method. Simenauer & Carroll found that two-thirds of men try pick-ups and one-third claim that a majority of women they approach respond favorably. Three-fourths of women say they are willing to be picked up. The most likely type of woman to pick up is between 25-34 years old, while the least likely is someone in her early 20's. High income professional men are more likely to attempt a pick-up than their low-income counterparts.

Laurie is a 24 year old seamstress. "I admire guys who try to pick me up. I know it takes some guts. As long as a guy isn't obnoxious, I take it as a compliment. One time I saw a cute guy at a shoe store who really turned me on Normally I don't have the nerve but this guy was too good to miss. I asked him if he thought the prices were reasonable and we wound up getting into a long conversation for the rest of the afternoon. We never did pick up any shoes. We picked each other up instead."

Perry is a 36 year old podiatrist. "I was moving into a new apartment one day and spotted a pretty girl watching me. I asked if she wanted to help and surprise! She said yes. She did the work of three guys from Bekins. I rewarded her a hundredfold the next few months with dinners, shows and some wonderful times."

## OTHER PLACES TO MEET PEOPLE

Simenauer & Carroll's survey revealed that approximately four out of every ten single people meet someone attractive at either bars, singles clubs or dating services. The next three chapters are devoted to these options.

# LIFE ON THE MEAT RACK: HOW TO SURVIVE A SINGLES BAR

"Singles bars are the pits" is a frequent refrain of single people. Sweet and gentle women turn into raving banshees when the topic comes up. Most singles fall into three categories: 1) those who have never gone to singles bars; 2) those who stopped going because they never met anyone "worthwhile"; and 3) those who go because they can't think of anywhere better to meet people.

Why is there such universal distaste for bars? A good answer from a male perspective is provided by Tom a 45 year old insurance adjuster. "After I separated from my wife, I decided to go down to one of the more notorious pick-up joints to see if the rules had changed. After all, back in the days when I was still a callow fellow, there was no such thing as women's lib. I figured that the new bar scene would be liberated—the women would be putting the make on the guys. Boy, was I wrong! Nothing had changed in 25 years.

"Immediately I noticed that segregation was still in effect. I'm not talking about racial segregation—I mean sexual. All the guys were lined up three deep at the bar. There were a few ladies at the bar—very few. Ninety percent of the women were sitting at tables in the dark corners of the room. I guess they were hiding out from all the make-out artists. These women were as chicken as they were in my early single days. They all had one or two bodyguards (friends) with them to protect their virtue.

"Some of the guys weren't too cool—they would stare

at the women they found attractive. But they were the minority. Most of the guys were secretly scanning the women out of the corners of their eyes. They were putting on a great show of laughing and joking with their buddies, but I knew what was really going on. They felt the same need to score that I felt when I was a kid. Most of the guys handled the pressure the same way I used to—they got bombed. It takes two or three drinks before you're ready to take a chance. You know that all the women at the tables are going to be engrossed in conversation. Why is it that women in bars are always talking non-stop to girlfriends. Don't they realize how difficult it is for a guy to intrude on a conversation?

"The first guy I noticed make his move was all smiles, all confidence. I couldn't hear what his line was, but whatever it was it didn't work. She probably told him she was only there to listen to the music.. How come so many women come down to a singles bar with wall-to-wall men in order to listen to the music?

"The poor schmuck then had to make the long walk back to the bar, convinced that all eyes in the place were on him in his moment of humiliation. He made a good show of it when he got back to his friends. He cracked a few jokes about 'stuck-up broads'. But I could tell he was hurting—he didn't return to the fray until after another drink.

"My heart went out to the guy. He had the guts to try again a few more times and eventually wound up hitting on someone. Who knows? Maybe he got lucky that night. What's sad is all the guys who chickened out. They ordered one drink and then left. Others got rejected a couple of times and decided to move on to greener pastures. I was content to be the observer that night. I wasn't bloodied until future engagements. Boy, do I hate singles bars!"

Judy is an attractive 22 year old, slim and blond. You'd think she would do well in singles bars but she doesn't. Why does she go? "I get bored on Saturday nights when I don't have a date. Who wants to watch television when everyone else is having fun? I'll call up a friend or two (or vice-versa) and we'll get all decked out and go out on the town.

"The best singles bars are the ones with the live bands. Even if all you meet all night are jerks, at least the music is good. We arrive early so we can find ourselves a table. We order drinks and listen to the band tune up. Eventually the music starts and the place starts filling up. A lot of guys are just standing around. I don't know why they don't come up to our table. We're all fairly attractive and are ready to boogie. Some nerd keeps eye-balling me—I know what's on his mind. He'd better find somebody else.

"I can't believe that with all the guys in this place no one has come up to our table. There are uglier girls than us on that dance floor! We're having a nice time talking but we can do that at home. Annette gets antsy and says she's gonna ask a guy to dance. I sure envy her. She's not the kind to wait for things to happen. Me, I'm a little conservative. I don't care what they say, most guys can't handle an assertive woman. I let the guy come to *me* and if he's cute and not too phony and makes a good living, then I'm available to get to know him better.

"Some guy comes up and asks Barbara to dance. He's not much, but I guess Barbara's desperate, so she goes out on the dance floor with him. The guy's buddy comes over a minute later—what a creep! I tell him "maybe later" and he walks off kind of dejectedly. I hate to hurt his feelings but I can't stand beards.

"I can't believe that only one guy has come up to me so far. At least I'm not fat like a lot of the ladies around here. Annette and Barbara don't seem to be hitting it off with anyone so I suggest that we move on across the street. On our way out a cute guy starts rapping with me—where was he the last two hours? He wants to follow me out but I've got my girlfriends to consider. I give him my number. I wonder if he'll call me. Probably not. Those bastards all have wallets full of numbers they never call."

People complain endlessly about the sordidness of bars, but one positive feature should not be overlooked: they are loaded with single people. Women complain that a majority of guys who go to bars are: 1) married, 2) living with a woman, 3) from out of town, 4) looking for a one-night stand, 5) jerks, 6) alcoholics, or 7) all of the above. This may be true, but it's also a fact that numerous attractive single men go to bars looking for an intimate relationship. The other thing to realize about singles bars is that they are the one place where the rules of etiquette make it easiest to approach someone. The same people who are aghast if you approach them on the street or in an elevator are usually friendly in a bar. From the standpoint of rejection, singles bars are probably the safest place to initiate contact with someone of the opposite sex.

There are two kinds of singles bars: conversation bars and dance bars (sometimes called discos). The difference between the two should be fairly obvious. The music at conversation bars is not so loud as to drown out people's voices. It serves as a pleasant backdrop for meeting people. In dance bars the music clearly comes first. It may be rock, it may be disco, but it's always loud. Conversation is limited to those who are exceptionally keen of hearing and have powerful lungs.

Which type is best for meeting people? If your goal is more than having fun and making casual contact with dance partners—if you really want to get to know someone —go to a conversation bar. If you prefer dance bars, be aware that there are two kinds: one has live music, the other has records or tapes. If you have a choice, go to the one with live music. The band takes a 15-20 minute break each hour, during which conversation is possible. Many singles claim that with the live music dance bar, you have the best of both worlds: great music, the fun of dancing, and good conversation with interesting new people.

One problem many singles have, particularly those from the Fred Astaire-Ginger Rogers era, is how to dance to modern music. Some feel very insecure on the dance floor during fast tunes because there aren't any set steps like the fox trot, rhumba, or waltz. Many a middle-aged single has asked, "How do I know if I'm doing it right?" This is a foolish question because with rock or disco you literally can't dance the wrong step. All you need to do is move to the beat and try not to bump or hit anyone. The problem is that many singles are inhibited and afraid of looking foolish. The way to get over this fear is to study the dancers on the floor and try to find someone who *doesn't* look ridiculous. This is an impossible task because to dance to modern music is to appear foolish. So don't worry about it. Go out on the dance floor and intentionally look stupid. People will compliment you on how uninhibited and original you are!

Simon is a 19 year old college student. "Throughout

high school, I only danced the slow numbers. I never had the nerve to shake to the fast music like everyone else. One night in the dorm I decided to see if booze might loosen me up. I rarely drink so after two screwdrivers I was snockered. I went out to the dance on campus and had the time of my life. I must have thought I was John Travolta! All I had to do was loosen up and move to the music and I was a hit."

Age is an important consideration. Check out the bars in your community and find out the kind of music they feature. Contemporary music, for example, is likely to attract a very young (18-35) crowd. Organ music attracts middle-aged and older singles. Style of clothing can also be important. Observe what other people in the bar are wearing and dress accordingly. Otherwise you may stand out like a sore thumb and attract the wrong kind of attention.

What if you don't drink? There's nothing wrong with ordering soft drinks or coffee. Rich is a 41 year old reformed alcoholic. "When I gave up booze I figured that was the end of visits to bars. I'd have to find another place to socialize. One night a friend insisted that I accompany him to what used to be our favorite hangout. Charlie, the bartender, welcomed me like a long-lost brother. 'Your usual, Rich?' he asked. I answered 'Milk'. His jaw dropped but he served me with a straight face. Later that night I had a few cups of coffee. I was shocked to discover that I had a great time without alcohol to loosen me up. Now I can meet people in any bar without booze and without embarrassment. Sometimes I feel a little sinful and try something stronger than milk, like club soda."

## TIPS FOR WOMEN

What can a woman do to meet that special man in a bar?

1. Sit at the bar, not at a table in a dark corner. This makes you accessible. Many more men will initiate contact with you and you can afford to be more choosy.

2. Go by yourself. Your friends are protecting you from meeting nice guys as well as losers.

3.  Don't be naive and believe everything a man tells you. It's true that men in bars frequently lie about their marital status, love life, location, etc.

4.  Initiate contact. Many women complain that the "good guys" at the end of the bar are usually shy, while the ones who come over and flirt are the jerks and makeout artists. This is often true, but there's no law against walking over and introducing yourself.

5.  Learn to say no. If a guy is not your type, you're not doing him a favor by tolerating him. Let him know that you'd prefer talking to someone else. If the guy can't take no for an answer and gets obnoxious, tell the bartender. If that doesn't work, leave. Make sure he doesn't follow you into a dark, deserted parking lot. If necessary, ask another guy in the bar who is more gentlemanly to escort you to your car. That's a good ice-breaker, by the way, for meeting that shy, attractive guy at the end of the bar. He will be flattered to be asked to be your knight in shining armor.

### TIPS FOR MEN

What can a man do to meet the right woman in a singles bar?

1.  Understand why women are often defensive in bars. They have good reason to be. If a woman is hostile or unfriendly when you approach her, don't take it personally. You may have been preceded by some jerk. Another possibility is that she just has a rotten disposition. In that case be glad you were rejected.

2.  Initiate contact with many women, not just one. Bill, a 27 year old software salesman, shared his technique for meeting women at discos. "I have a rule that I have to dance with five different attractive women and memorize their names. Sometimes I'm lucky and the first five I ask all say yes. Other times I have to ask ten or more. After dancing with five attractive women, I have the luxury of choosing the one who is the most attractive, or the most friendly, or

a combination of both. If we don't hit it off, I still have four others to choose from."

3.    If you find someone you like, try to pin her down on when you will see her again. If you only take down her telephone number, there is a good chance you'll never see her again.

Singles bars are not dens of iniquity, despite their reputation. Be careful not to overgeneralize about the kind of people that go there. The same people you meet at work, at church, on the beach, and at parties are also likely to occasionally go to singles bar. Rather than write off the most obvious place to meet singles, take a chance and attend a bar. Many people have met their husband, wife or lover in a bar.

# SINGLES GROUPS

What could be easier than walking into a room of people gathered because they're single and want to meet someone special? There are literally thousands of singles groups throughout the United States. Some are even international. They sponsor an incredible variety of enjoyable activities. Some groups are specialized. They are devoted to one activity, like ballroom dancing or skiing. Others sponsor a host of activities, including parties, dances, dinners, picnics, sports, lectures and discussions.

Surprisingly, only a small percentage of the population attends singles groups. This is because of the widespread belief that only losers go to these groups. This is an unfair generalization. Of course, there are many losers at singles groups, but the same holds true for almost any other place you can meet people. The only sure-fire way to avoid losers is to stay home.

Another reason that people are reluctant to attend singles groups is that they fear only "swingers" attend and activities end in orgies. This image (to the chagrin of some members) is totally unfounded.

It's entertaining to listen to people at singles groups discuss why they are there. Few admit to being lonely. They usually don't even acknowledge that they hope to meet a person of the opposite sex. "I'm here to meet *people*" is the standard reply, as if they value platonic relationships as much as they do romantic ones. That's baloney. Most people don't go to singles groups to form casual friendships, although this

32

is certainly a valued by-product. They are looking for love and romance. They fear that they are the only ones, however, and that they will scare people off if they come on too strongly.

Perhaps they're right. If you go to singles groups, by all means play along with the games if you wish. You can pretend that you're there because there's nothing on television that night. If you want to have some fun, however, tell everyone you're there to fall in love. Some people will look at you funny, but others will be favorably impressed by your admitting to why most of them are there.

One common mistake people make is to go to a singles group once, not meet anyone attractive, and never return. Several thousand different people may attend a particular group over the course of a year, but only a tiny percentage attend any one meeting. You need to check a group out several times before making any firm conclusion about the membership.

A further advantage to attending the same group several times is that you begin to recognize people from previous meetings and feel more comfortable. The first time attending a group can be scary. After a while, however, you begin to feel part of the group and find it easier to initiate contact. Others will feel more comfortable approaching you as well.

The easiest way to meet people at a singles group is to volunteer to help. There are numerous chores that need to be done: making the coffee, tending bar, moving the furniture, cleaning up, publicity, mailings, etc. In addition to volunteering for specific jobs, you may also offer the use of your home for a party. Many groups schedule infrequent social events because too few of the members are willing to open up their homes to strangers. If you are unafraid, let people know that your home is available.

Joining the board of directors of a singles group can also pay off. You will become a "big cheese" and a member of the "in-crowd". Heide is a 38 year old hairdresser. "I used to resent the clannishness of my singles club. They were always laughing, easily made contact with new people and never looked alone and forlorn in a corner. One night they announced a need to replace a departing member of the steering committee. I volunteered and immediately felt a part of the action. Now I'm part of the inner circle and love it."

Joining a singles organization is usually easy and inexpensive. Being placed on a mailing list is free or costs a few dollars. You usually don't even have to join a club since many of their events are open to the general public.

How do you find out about singles clubs in your community? The easiest way is through your local church, which either sponsors a singles group or can refer you to a church that does. If you are Catholic, write to Separated & Divorced Catholics, 5 Park Street, Boston, MA, or call your local church to join the nearest chapter. If you are not only Catholic but also under 35, write to the Catholic Alumni Club International, 76 14th Street, North Tonawanda, New York 14120.

Virtually every Jewish Community Center sponsors activities for singles. Likewise for Unitarian churches. Protestant churches of every denomination usually have singles organizations, as do Mormons. Many of these church groups are wide open to the public and have no religious requirements. Even atheists are often welcome. The Unitarian singles groups are particularly appropriate because Unitarians don't have a set of dogmas. Theoretically anyone qualifies.

Parents Without Partners has chapters all over the United States. To qualify for membership, you must be single and have a living son or daughter. Custody of the child is not a requirement. PWP sponsors a wide variety of events through the month. Some of these events are for adults only, while others are for the entire family. For more information, contact your local chapter or write to: PWP International Headquarters, 7910 Woodmont Avenue, Washington, D.C. 20014.

Bachelors 'n Bachelorettes is a singles square dancing club with chapters throughout the nation. Beginners are welcome (there are instructors for that purpose). Again, you may contact your local chapter or write to Bob Wildman, Bachelors 'n Bachelorettes International, 5214 Ledgewood Road, Southgate, CA 90280. Tall Club International may be contacted at 920 Dallas Federal Savings & Trust, 8333 Douglas Street, Douglas, Texas 75225. To find out about other singles clubs, call your local newspaper or read the calendar section devoted to meetings of organizations.

Below are positive and negative comments about singles groups. Roy is a 28 year old sanitary worker. "I attend singles groups semi-regularly (twice a month on the average) and have met many fine people of both sexes. When I go, I don't expect to meet my 'true love'. I do anticipate having a good time, however. Occasionally someone cute comes along and I date her."

Irene is a 25 years old public relations consultant. "My one experience at a singles group was a disaster. All these old farts swooped down on me like I was a movie star or something. I'm not interested in dating someone as old as my grandfather!"

Margaret is a 44 year old store clerk. "I love to dance so I attend almost all the dances sponsored by local singles clubs. The music is great and occasionally I wind up dating someone new."

Hank is a 37 year old fireman; Cindy is a 36 year old insurance adjuster. "We met each other through a singles volleyball club."

Brian is a 48 year old dermatologist. "All the girls at singles groups are fuglies (fat and ugly)."

Nancy is 39 years old and unemployed. "I was really shy the first time I attended a singles group. It seemed to me that everyone was cliquish and I was an outsider. I kept coming, however, because I was going crazy staying at home. Now newcomers probably think that I'm cliquish since I'm always in the middle of a group of friends at singles events."

Ben is a 64 year old retired industrial engineer. "I get tired of all the ladies bitching about how their ex-husbands 'done me wrong'. I think most of them need to join therapy groups, not singles groups."

Noreen is a 40 year old artist and Lorenzo is a 40 year old psychotherapist. "We met as members of the board of directors of our singles club. One day we spent several hours recording tapes for a dance sponsored by the club and before we knew it we fell in love."

Simenauer & Carroll discovered that 14% of men and 18% of women meet most of their dates through singles clubs. The average person is middle-aged, so don't expect to meet people in their twenties or early thirties at most singles clubs, unless the group is athletic in nature or is limited to

35

people under 35.

# DATING SERVICES

An alternative to non-profit singles groups are the professional dating services. These range in price from free to hundreds of dollars. As in the case of singles groups, you will run into all kinds of single people, some winners and some losers.

**TELEPHONE DATING**

These are among the cheapest of dating services. Often there is only a small monthly charge ($10 and up). Because of the low cost, telephone dating services often boast of large memberships. You are usually given the first names, ages, towns and telephone numbers of a list of people of the opposite sex.

Once you have that list, you are on your own. You can call as many prospects on your list as you wish or be passive and wait for the phone to ring. Some typical opinions of telephone dating follow.

Marianne is a 38 year old systems analyst. "I have met several nice men through the club. Nothing serious has developed as of yet but I'm having a good time."

Otis is a 28 year old seeking employment. "I'm going steady with a girl I met through telephone dating. I particularly liked the idea that she called me originally and not the other way around."

Laverne is an 18 year old student. "Joining telephone dating was the worst thing I ever did! I felt like my phone number was on the wall of every men's room in town. I got

18 to 19 calls a day until I had my phone number changed."

Richard, a 48 years attorney, had this experience: "I was very disappointed. Many of the phone numbers I called were disconnected or the ladies that answered were very defensive."

## LONELY HEARTS CLUBS

These are also very inexpensive ($5 to $25). You receive lists of singles together with their addresses and photographs. It's up to you to correspond through the mail with the people you want to meet. A major criticism of these clubs is that the lists may be several years old.

## COMPUTER DATING

This was the craze during the late sixties and early seventies. Computer dating is still quite popular throughout the United States. The cost can be minimal ($25 to $35), or can be quite expensive, depending on the company. The procedure is to fill out a questionnaire describing your physical appearance, personality, hobbies, interests, etc. and what you seek in an ideal mate. Your political, religious and sexual attitudes are often included also. The computer matches you with others whose answers are compatible with yours.

Tony, a 58 years old physical education teacher, had this to say about computer dating: "I dated 5 girls via the computer. I am still dating one of them."

Olivia is a 22 year old cocktail waitress. "I met my fiance through computer dating. Was I surprised! I only did it as a lark."

Paul is a 27 year old house painter. "I think computer dating is a rip-off. I dated two women through the service and both were physically unattractive.

Rochelle is a 48 year old seeking employment. "I met a few losers through computer dating."

## PERSONAL ADS

Personal ads are prominently displayed in newspapers and magazines around the country, although only 1% of singles find their partners this way. Back in the sixties, only avante-garde, radical newspapers like the *Berkeley Barb* accepted personal ads, but now even the most respectable of papers solicit them.

Due to the law of supply and demand, women usually do better than men when it comes to personal ads. Very few women feel comfortable placing an ad, so those that do receive numerous responses. Sometimes these number in the hundreds! Women can often afford to be selective and choose the cream of the crop. Mary, a 51 year old cosmetologist, has dated several men through personal ads and gives the following suggestions for women:

1. Never give your last name, address, or phone number in a personal ad. Have the newspaper collect the responses for you.

2. In your ad, say who you are and what you're looking for. Be specific and honest. Otherwise you're wasting your time and your money.

3. After reading all the responses, write to the guys who sound most attractive. Include a current photo of yourself and request one of him.

4. Meet the guy for the first time at a public place, like a restaurant.

Alfred, 24 year old bookkeeper, expressed the following about personal ads: "I have been very disappointed. I responded to several ads but never got a response from any of the women. I guess they got so many replies that they never got around to answering me."

Larry is a 27 year old weightlifting instructor: "I was surprised by the volume of response to my ad—38 girls. I don't spend Saturday nights alone anymore."

Susie is a 25 year old writer: "I met my husband through an ad I placed in the local paper."

Karen is a 43 year old physician. "I've never dated the same man twice from personal ads."

## PHOTO DATING

This is often more expensive than either telephone or computer dating. However, being able to see what someone looks like before going out may be worth the added expense (approximately $150).

Along with the photograph, there is a fact sheet that gives you vital statistics about the person as well as other information such as hobbies and interests.

Ron, a 50 year old cook, had this to say about photo dating: "I was very pleased with some of the women I dated through the club. It sure beat going out on blind dates through the computer."

Elaine is a 23 year old dental assistant. "I was disappointed that people often didn't look that much like their photo. I guess if you photograph Godzilla enough times, you'll get at least one good snapshot."

## VIDEO DATING

This process involves going through several photo albums full of members. Next to the photo is a fact sheet, as with photo dating. Once you have narrowed down your choices, you may request to see video tapes of the people you like. Each tape is a five minute interview.

When you select someone for a date, you don't get their phone number until after they've also had the chance to come down and read your fact sheet and watch your videotape. On the other hand, if someone selects *you* for a date, your phone number is kept confidential until you've had the chance to check them out. Some differences from photo dating are:

1.  The cost is usually more.
2.  You get a more accurate picture of how people look when you see them continuously for five minutes (up close, far away, from different camera angles).
3.  You also can see their body language, poise, facial expressions, gestures, etc.
4.  You get to hear them talk about themselves also.
5.  You don't have to worry about unattractive people calling you, because your phone number is only given to people you want to date.
6.  You don't have to worry about rejection either, since the only time you get to call someone is when they agree in advance to go out with you.
7.  Likewise you don't have to reject anyone since the only people who get your phone number are those whom you find attractive.

For women, video dating is a very safe way to meet men, since rapists are unlikely to join a club where their videotape can be turned over to the police. For men, it's a real treat since a good percentage of the time the women initiate contact. The feeling of safety and assurance that they won't be rejected encourages women to be far more liberated and initiate contact.

Kirk, a 31 year old office manager, shared the following experience. "Before I joined video dating, I had never been chosen by a woman for a date. Needless to say I was delighted with all the attractive women who selected me. Even when I found a woman to be unattractive, I still was happy she chose me—it did a lot for my ego. I also found that my shyness didn't work against me in video dating. I wasn't afraid to call good looking women because I was promised in advance they would say yes to going out with me."

Joline is a 30 year old architect. "I used to avoid asking guys out before video dating. This has been a very liberating experience for me. It's like walking into a candy store. It's mind-boggling to have all those attractive men to choose from. I was guaranteed that they were all single, local, had a steady job and were safe. I wouldn't be caught dead approaching a man in a singles bar, but with video dating, I was not inhibited in the slightest."

Barry is a 46 year old sheet metal worker. "I thought video dating was a rip-off. All that money and I never did meet the right girl. For the same price I could have gone to Hawaii for a vacation."

## MATCHMAKING

While video and computer dating utilize the latest in modern technology, the age-old art of matchmaking still flourishes in the twentieth century. The matchmaker brings people together on the basis of impressions and information gathered during interviews with clients.

The main objection to matchmaking is that if you have a difficult time figuring out who is right for you, how can another person, who knows even less about your needs and taste, do better?

Sara, a 57 year old bank teller, had this to say about matchmaking: "I met a fine gentleman through a matchmaker. It really works!"

Donald is a 36 year old radio engineer. "I paid $400 for three matches. None of the ladies were my type."

## LUXURY SOCIAL CLUBS

These clubs profess to have the answer for those who like to party but are leery of running into losers. Luxury social clubs claim to have "high-quality clientele" (which usually means beautiful and wealthy) and to provide pleasant surroundings (yachts, mansions, etc.) for meeting them.

Ted, a 30 years old bus driver, shared the following experience with a luxury social club. "I went to a few events but didn't see anyone I found attractive."

Joan is a 35 years old reading specialist. "I asked for my money back ($600) but didn't succeed in getting it."

## CHOOSING THE RIGHT DATING SERVICE

Not all dating services are established or reputable. One high-priced matchmaker/computer dating service that charged $500 went bankrupt after the owner ran off to Mexico with all the money. He didn't even pay his own employees. Another high-priced service ($1000) is presently being investigated by the State Attorney General's Office for possible fraud. Be sure to investigate all of the dating services in your area before making up your mind on which one(s) to join. Consider the following criteria:

1. Number of people in the service
2. Cost of membership
3. Duration of membership
4. Privileges of membership
5. Hidden or extra costs
6. Screening process of prospective members
7. Confidentiality
8. Amount of time they have been in the business
9. What the Better Business Bureau, news media, etc., have to say about the dating service
10. What is guaranteed in writing, as opposed to verbal promises.

# MAKING TIME FOR
# MEETING PEOPLE

You may want to go where the ducks are but feel that you don't have the time or energy. There are three main reasons why you might have difficulty: 1) you are a single parent; 2) you take care of aged or invalid parents or relatives; 3) you are too busy making money. Below are suggestions for dealing with these situations.

## SINGLE PARENTS
Working full-time and raising one or more children can be a nightmare, particularly if the children are very young. Single parents have a tendency to go off the deep end and attempt to replace the missing parent. This is impossible. Effective parenting is quite a challenge even when you're splitting the responsibility with a spouse. Unfortunately, divorced parents frequently feel guilty of depriving their children of a "stable home" with two parents and, therefore, overcompensate. Widowed parents may also feel obligated to substitute for the missing parent.

If you're a single parent and suffer from this problem, you need to realize several things:

1.	Yes, it's sad that your children now only live with one parent. As a general rule two parents can do a better job than one. Your kids may suffer somewhat because of the loss of one parent. On the other hand, it's better to live in a happy home with one parent than an unhappy one with two. Sadly, too many people stay in

43

miserable marriages for the children's sake. Children do not benefit from living in homes where there is a great deal of frustration, hostility and resentment.

2.    To a large extent, your ability to be an effective parent will depend on whether or not your own needs are met. If you're unhappy, the odds are that your children will be also. Unless you have some stimulation in your life, you're likely to be depressed a great deal. This can be very contagious to your kids.

3.    Your children may feel frustrated, fearful, or resentful if you frequently go out and leave them with the baby-sitter. That's because they don't realize that it is definitely to their advantage as well as yours to have your needs for companionship and romance met. Otherwise your batteries will run down and you may have nothing to give them except a relationship with a lifeless shell. Don't allow your children to run your life. For better or worse, you are in charge and must make the decisions.

Maria is a 28 years old mother of two. "I tried to go out a few times, but it got to be too much of a hassle. I was heartbroken to see my children cry when I'd go out for the evening. They had already suffered so much from the loss of their father (Maria is a widow). Also it was humiliating to have a guy show up at my door and witness the tantrums the kids would throw about my leaving. Finally, I just stopped going out altogether.

"On one hand, it was very comfortable to stay home each night and relax after a hard day's work. Gradually, however, I started feeling so isolated and lonely. My kids were both under six so I couldn't relate to them other than as a mommy. I was starved for adult companionship.

"One day I sat down and had a long conversation with myself. I faced up to the fact that I was very resentful towards my children for keeping me a prisoner in my own home. Sometimes I actually hated them! I was so ashamed. But then I realized that my children weren't to blame—I was the culprit. Kids are by nature selfish and demanding. It's up to the parents to draw the line and look out for themselves. I was foolish to expect my kids to understand my needs.

"I'm dating at least once a week now and usually go out to socialize at least one other night. The babysitting is expensive but I'm willing to sacrifice other things that I used to think were more important. I'm now much happier. I don't feel like I'm on an emotional treadmill anymore. And, of course, as I should have been able to predict, my kids are happier, too."

## BABYSITTING

Finding a babysitter usually is one of the greatest problems single parents have to face. Take advantage of the opportunity to share babysitting responsibilities with other single parents. You can find people with the same needs as yours in any neighborhood or at work, school, or church. Singles clubs are full of single parents who would be willing to trade babysitting nights with you.

Cooperative babysitting groups are a relatively new trend catching fire. If there are no such groups in your community, why not start one? All you need to do is spread the word to single parents about your desire to organize such a group. You can easily do this by placing notices on bulletin boards at work, supermarkets, or churches. You can also insert free items in church or club newsletters. You might call your local newspaper and tell them about the concept of babysitting cooperatives. They might even do a story featuring your efforts. That way you not only get your babysitting needs met but become famous in the bargain!

A fringe benefit of sharing babysitting responsibilities with other single parents is the emotional support you can provide one another. No one can fully understand what you're going through except other single parents. The opportunity to talk to someone who can empathize with you is quite a blessing. Don't be afraid to ask for more than babysitting support. Single parents will be happy to listen to you with understanding as long as you're willing to do the same for them.

Also, don't be afraid to ask for babysitting help from relatives. Grandparents are usually a soft touch, while aunts, uncles, cousins, godparents, former in-laws, etc., can often be persuaded also.

Your ex-spouse is another possibility. Women usually win custody of the kids (sometimes after a vicious court battle) only to discover that they lost: their ex-spouses go out and have all the fun while they stay home to wash the diapers. If you're a single mother with custody, consider the option of occasionally "unloading" the children on their father. Try not to allow resentments to blind you to the fact that in most cases your children will profit from more exposure to their father.

Darlene is a 35 year old inventory-taker. "I fought hard to get custody of the kids. Our divorce was a bitter struggle and I made sure I won most of the battles. I was required to let Gary see the children on Saturdays—but that was it. Gary was a rotten person, in my opinion, and I wanted to limit his contact with my boys to the bare minimum. I didn't want them to inherit his foul disposition and hang-ups.

"Unfortunately, the child support was non-existent (Gary was chronically out of work) so I couldn't afford to pay a babysitter. I stayed home each night even though I was dying to get out of the house and meet men.

"Gradually I got over my resentments toward Gary and began to understand some of his problems and even feel sorry for him. He was very lonely and missed the children deeply. I started to take advantage of his free time by dropping off the kids once or twice a week. He was delighted and the kids liked it, too. I must confess I was a little jealous about that. I came to realize that Gary wasn't such a bad guy after all and that he gave the boys things that I couldn't. There was no way I could play the role of daddy as well as he could. Now Gary and I are even friends. I wouldn't ever marry him again—that would be a calamity! But I'm discovering that co-parenting is great."

One option that many single parents overlook is the children taking care of themselves. Joe is a 39 year old single father. "I was always afraid to leave my kids alone. They're somewhat sneaky and I was afraid they'd experiment with drugs, cigarettes, booze, and sex. So I watched them like a hawk. Later on I found out that all my efforts had been for naught. My girls (Mary is 14 and Charlene is 12) had both had "hits" on marijuana at school but didn't like it. They only did it so they wouldn't be called "chicken". They also had ample opportunity to use other drugs, like speed, downers, and coke, not to mention booze and sex. My kids just weren't interested. My policing wouldn't have prevented them doing all the things I had nightmares about.

"Now I go out any night I feel the desire and leave the girls behind to take care of themselves. Maybe they smoke cigarettes behind my back, but they can do that at school anyway. I call home frequently to allay my fears, but I have fun anyway."

One of the great fears of hard-working single parents is that they won't be able to give enough time to their children. It's important to realize that children need quality time, not quantity. Studies have compared working mothers with those who stay at home. No correlation was found between effective parenting and whether or not the parent worked. Working mothers were able to satisfy their children's needs for love, guidance and security as effectively as those who were full-time parents.

Another worry that plagues single mothers is whether or not any man will ever be willing to marry them. Robert Weiss reveals in *Marital Separation* that single mothers are just as likely to find another husband as someone who never has had children.

## AGED OR INVALID PARENTS AND RELATIVES

These can be even more of a burden than young children. This may sound callous, but the tragic fact is that many single people feel forced to take care of parents or siblings to the exclusion of their own social needs.

Agnes is a 52 year old widow with no children. "My dad is 75 and has been very dependent on me physically since his stroke last year. If anything, his psychological dependence is even greater, since my mom has been dead for four years. We'd get into such horrible fights whenever I went out for the evening that I finally gave up and abandoned my social life altogether. After developing an ulcer, I decided to take my doctor's advice and go out and have a good time. I hired the neighbor's teenager to watch over dad a couple of nights a week while I went out and had a ball. Now I'm engaged to be married!"

Escaping from home is difficult for many single people who have dependent loved ones. It must be done, however, and *frequently*. If you find that guilt is preventing you from meeting someone special, tell yourself the following over and over:

- I have a right to be happy.
- My needs are important too.
- I can't give what I don't have.
- No one has a right to demand that I live a miserable life.

Once you emancipate yourself, you will be able to enjoy life. You will also find that subconscious resentments towards your dependents will disappear.

### TOO BUSY MAKING MONEY?

Workaholism is a frequent problem among single people. Work enables you to escape the fear, loneliness and boredom that often plague singles. Unfortunately, it doesn't help you get your romantic needs met.

It's important to get your priorities straight. What is more important: to have a great deal of money or meet a special person? If you answer the former, the obvious question is, "How much fun will I have spending all that money on myself?" Most of us enjoy doing things with others more than by ourselves. The joys of travel, movies, fine restaurants, concerts, camping, hiking, etc., are usually enhanced by company. If you find that you're spending so much time on your business or profession that your social life is suffering, do the following exercise.

### EXERCISE
1. What is the minimum amount of money you must earn to be happy? $_____
2. How many hours can you cut from your work schedule and still earn that amount? _____
3. Rearrange your schedule so you are working a minimum number of hours and socializing the maximum amount of time. You may have to change the hours of operation of your business or profession or come in late once a week. Another possibility is to work overtime a few days to free yourself on others.

If you can't cut your hours and earn enough money, there are other options. For example:

1.   Delegate responsibilities to subordinates. Most "indispensable people find that they are deluding themselves if they put it to a sincere test. Sidney is a 59 year old car dealer. "I put in 70 hour weeks for many years. With car dealers going under right and left, I didn't think I could afford to go out and have fun. Then I had a heart attack and was hospitalized. While I was gone, sales were almost as high as when I was running the show. I lost some money lying on my back while others ran the store, but we still were in the black. Now I still have a tendency to work too hard but I'm taking my doctor's advice most of the time. I take it easy more often and I also find the time to go out and party occasionally."

2.   Subcontract some of your work. Arnie is a 40 year old general contractor. "I'm a jack of all trades. I do excellent work and am very efficient. By doing almost all of the electrical, plumbing and carpentry myself, I made good money. One summer I spent a week in Mexico City. Everything was beautiful and fascinating but I was very disappointed. I realized something was missing—a woman to share all this. I made a resolution never again to go alone on a vacation.
      "When I got back home I started hiring people to do some of the work. I lost some money in the beginning and went through a few subcontractors. Then I found a guy who was talented, versatile, hard-working, dependable and worked cheap. He was a gold mine. Now I subcontract a good part of my business and have plenty of time to date. And I'm still making good money."

3.   Buy labor-saving equipment. Barbara is a 42 year old newpaper editor. "Ours is a small town paper, so we operate on a shoestring budget. We can't afford to buy all the fancy hardware that the big city papers have. I found that I was working myself to death and didn't have time to meet men socially. The solution was to

buy an old dictaphone. I got it for next to nothing. I found that I could dictate feature stories a lot faster than I could type them. I hired an 18 year old college student to transcribe the stories. This enabled me to go home a little earlier once or twice a week. I was able to eat dinner, relax, and then go out and mingle. That's all it took for me to meet Ollie." (Ollie is Barbara's husband.)

# INITIATING CONTACT

Don is a 47 year old graphic artist. "I see all kinds of attractive women—on the subway, in bars, jogging in the park. The trouble is that they never say Hi to me and I'm too scared to approach them."

Sally is a 24 year old stewardess. "Why is it that guys are so shy?" she complains. "If I go to a bar dressed to kill, obviously I'm there to meet guys. So what's so scary about saying hello? I don't bite."

Don and Sally are in the same predicament: they violate the third and most important rule of the Numbers Game: Initiate Contact. They and millions of other singles are like ships passing in the night. Who knows how many beautiful relationships have never taken place because both people were afraid to make the first move?

The $64,000 question, of course, is "Who should initiate contact?" According to Ethel, a 63 year old school teacher, "It's up to the men to initiate contact. It's a man's world and it's their responsibility to get the ball rolling." Ed, a 51 year old draftsman, disagrees. "What about all this talk of women's liberation. I'm tired of putting my ego on the line. Why can't women take the first step? They need us as much as we need them."

Ethel and Ed are doing what President Truman always promised to avoid: passing the buck. They are giving others the responsibility for meeting their needs. This is great if you can find somebody willing to do it. But most of us are not so lucky. The answer to the question of who should initiate contact is YOU. Don't depend on others to come up to you —they probably are just as afraid of rejection as you are. Remember this equation: One Shy Man + One Shy Woman = No Contact and No Relationship.

Many women refuse to initiate contact because they are convinced that "men don't like forward women." My interviews and conversations with hundreds of single men suggest the complete opposite: most men are quite flattered when women approach them. Simenauer & Carrol's survey confirmed this observation. They found that two-thirds of men think it's all right for women to ask men out for a date.

Sam, a 43 year old construction worker, is typical of many single men. "I've never had a woman approach me but if it happened I think it would be great—unless I had a heart attack from the surprise." Joe is a 29 year old law student. "Girls ask me out every once in a while. I think it's wonderful."

Why do women think that men don't appreciate forward women? I've asked this question many times and the response is usually the same: "I once asked a guy to dance and he said no. So you see, men don't like assertive women!" What many women don't realize is that the average man doesn't find the average woman to be attractive. Men are just as selective as women are. If they occasionally turn down a woman who approaches them, it doesn't necessarily mean they are against forward women.

Often the biggest hurdle on the road to a loving relationship is shyness. According to Arthur Wassmer, in his book *Making Contact*, "Shyness may be at once the most widespread and the least noticed psychological problem of Americans today. . . . As research has indicated, 40% or more of us experience shyness as a serious problem in our daily lives."

Jim is a good example. At social events, he goes to great lengths to stay away from people. When he crosses a room he walks around individuals or groups for fear of being drawn into conversation. He also avoids people's eyes. That way they're less likely to come over and talk to him. If he accidentally makes eye contact with someone, he quickly turns away.

No matter how much his feet hurt, Jim prefers to stand. That way he's less likely to be cornered. When he does sit down, he never shares a sofa, preferring his own chair. He sits as far away from people as possible and likes to have a coffee table in front of him.

Jim's body language is that of a fearful, closed person. When conversing, he crosses his arms and legs. He keeps his shoulders hunched and his head pointed down. When he talks, he looks away from people. He also avoids touching them like the plague. He limits physical contact to the beginning and end of a conversation and only if the other person initiates things. He never goes beyond a perfunctory handshake. He only allows contact with his fingers, never his palm. His handshake is limp and quick.

When people speak to him, Jim seldom nods in agreement or shakes his head in disagreement. He usually keeps his head rigidly in place. He also keeps a deadpan expression on his face. He usually doesn't smile, frown, wink or raise his eyebrows at anyone.

Jim is typical of millions of shy singles who seldom make good contact with attractive people of the opposite sex. If you share Jim's problem, make a strong effort to practice the following suggestions.

1.  Stay close to people physically. If you walk into a bar or party, sit or stand where most of the other people are. Whenever you walk around a room, pass as closely as you can to people without bumping into them. (On the other hand, intentionally bumping into people may be a good way to meet them. Just be gentle.)

2.  Ask people to sit down with you if you are conversing for more than a few minutes. That way you can both relax and feel comfortable. Sit together as closely as possible (without crowding one another). Try to remove barriers between you such as coffee tables or other people.

3.  Stand tall with your head up. If necessary, pretend that you're General Patton: be a little arrogant and even swagger when you walk into a room. Sometimes exaggerated behavior such as this can help break old, established patterns.

4.    Sit or stand with an open posture. Keep your arms and legs uncrossed.

5.    Lean towards people when they talk to you. This shows interest in what they're saying. Leaning back in your chair may come across as disapproval, boredom or disinterest.

6.    Maintain eye contact as much as possible, without staring. It isn't possible to simultaneously watch both of a person's eyes, so pick one. If you feel uncomfortable looking at an eye, then focus on an ear or forehead. As long as you're looking somewhere on a person's face, it appears that you're looking them in the eye.

**EXERCISE**

Ask a friend to help you learn how to maintain eye contact. Sit across from each other and look each other in the eye for two minutes. Both of you should keep silent during this exercise.

A variation is to take turns giving a monologue (one person does all the talking) for a specific length of time. The other person just listens, making sure to maintain eye contact.

You may find that you can't look someone in the eye for long without bursting into laughter. Laughing is a normal, nervous reaction, so don't give up. Keep practicing until you can maintain eye contact without laughing.

Practice both variations of this exercise frequently. Gradually increase the amount of time so that you can maintain steady eye contact for at least ten minutes.

7.    When conversing, use frequent head gestures. Nod when you agree and shake your head when you disagree. This lets others know your reaction to what they're saying. Nodding your head doesn't necessarily mean you agree with them. You are only indicating that you are following their comments closely and are interested.

8.    Remember to use facial expressions. A smile can

indicate that you feel happy, safe, or find someone attractive. It also indicates that you're open to meeting people. The most important thing to remember about smiling is that it probably makes you look more attractive. That's why photographers go to such lengths to get you to smile.

A frown can also be helpful, as long as it isn't your standard expression. A quizzical look communicates that you don't understand something. There are many other facial expressions that are also helpful in communicating your thoughts and feelings.

Women are often taught to avoid facial expressions for fear of wrinkles. Living a controlled, unemotional life is a heavy price to pay for preserving a youthful face. Proper skin care should enable you to look attractive and still have an expressive face.

9.    Observe a mime the next time you have a chance. Notice how much can be communicated by posture, movement, gestures and facial expressions. Start watching yourself and notice your body language. Don't make the mistake of having your words say that you're friendly and want to meet people while your body expresses the opposite.

10.   Reach out and touch someone, as the commercial goes. Handshakes are the easiest form of physical contact. Grasp the other person's entire hand (not just the fingers) and shake firmly (without overdoing it). Some people, particularly women, will only give you their fingers to grasp. You can be satisfied with this or jokingly complain that they are being stingy and should give you their entire hand.

If it feels comfortable, use both your hands simultaneously to shake one of theirs. Putting your arm around people or touching them gently on the knee or arm are also beneficial. Just be sure to observe if they are comfortable with the physical intimacy. Men, in particular, need to be careful to avoid offending a woman by touching her before she feels safe and comfortable. Women should be equally cautious. If a man has sex on his mind, touching him may encourage more forwardness than you would like.

## ETIQUETTE

You may fear that initiating contact is contrary to one of the rules of etiquette: Don't approach strangers. Certainly there is some validity to this fear. Earlier in the twentieth century, it was considered impolite to approach strangers except to ask directions or the time of day. "Gentlemen" and "ladies" were properly introduced; otherwise they didn't speak to each other. In polite society, you handed people your "card". Fortunately those days are over. It has become more socially acceptable to initiate contact and not just at social events. To overcome your resistance to initiating contact, you need to confront three fears:

1.   The fear of scaring someone. When you approach strangers, they have no way of knowing whether you are friendly or intend to rob, assault, rape or murder them. One way to minimize this fear is to meet people during daytime hours and where there are other people around. Approaching someone in a dark alley or on a secluded mountain path are guaranteed to freak them out.

2.   The fear of intruding. People lying out in the sun, reading a book or magazine, or engaged in some other enjoyable activity may not want you to interrupt. It's not that they don't find you attractive; they just don't want to be bothered at that particular moment. Unfortunately, it's often difficult to tell whether people are engrossed in what they're doing or are bored out of their minds. You just have to take your chances on intruding or miss out on countless opportunities to meet attractive people.

3.   The fear of negative labels. Men worry about being regarded as jerks or make-out artists if they initiate contact. Women worry about being labeled as "loose" or "on the make". The only way to avoid these negative labels is to stop initiating contact altogether. Otherwise, the price for meeting attractive people is

taking this risk.

Women are usually more reluctant to initiate contact than men. Ironically, they have less to fear. Women don't have to worry about scaring men, who normally are larger and stronger. There are some very shy or timid men who are easily intimidated, but they are a tiny minority. Most men feel flattered when women approach them. Even if they're engrossed in a pleasant activity, they welcome the intrusion!

It's important for both men and women to realize that there's one kind of stranger who will be delighted to have you initiate contact. This is the person looking for a loving relationship with someone just like you. You have no way of knowing in advance who this person is. The only way to avoid missing a golden opportunity is to approach every-one you find attractive. Of course, there are going to be times when you don't have the time, energy, or inclination to initiate contact. Certainly you have the right to let some op-portunities pass. But don't let this happen too often. If you're a selective single, there may not be that many chances, so make sure you take advantage of most of them.

### OPENING LINES

Do you fantasize that if you only had the perfect opening line (like they do in the movies), you'd never have to face rejection? I've seen ads for a book by Eric Webber called *100 Best Opening Lines*. Without even reading it, I would be willing to bet that all 100 lines in the book work. The reason is that all lines work—some of the time.

When lecturing on the topic of initiating contact, my favorite suggestion is to say, "Hi, I'm a jerk." The audi-ence gets a big kick out of it and they also get the point— that any line is better than no line at all. The only thing that doesn't work is silence.

The best line I've ever heard was delivered by a friend one night in a disco. Randy was wearing a tank top, shabby cutoffs, and filthy sneakers. He hadn't showered or shaved that day, either. We both spotted a beautiful woman sitting at the bar. A steady succession of guys noticed her, fell in love (or lust) and walked over to ask her to dance. All of them were rejected.

Randy nudged me and said he was going to dance

with her. I told him that he was crazy. Why would a beautiful woman dance with him when she was turning down neat, well-dressed, handsome men? Randy wouldn't listen. He walked over to the bar, spoke to her for a few seconds, and led her to the dance floor. I was flabbergasted. This had to be the greatest line in history.

Half an hour later, Randy rejoined me at our table. I asked, "How much did you pay her?" He answered, "I asked her if she would dance with an ugly man. She looked a little embarrassed but danced with me anyway. Later, when we returned to the bar, she asked me if I really thought I was ugly. I answered, 'Hell, no, but I had to get you off the damn stool, didn't I?'"

Randy had an outlandish, clever line that worked, but you really don't have to be creative. Simple lines work, too. One favorite with women is, "How are you doing?" There's nothing spectacular about it, but it isn't overly cute either. It has two main advantages. First, it's an easy question. She's almost certain to respond, which gets the conversation going. Second, it's safe, non-threatening and puts her at ease.

While any line can work, the best ones are spontaneous and tailor-made for the person you want to meet. Watch people closely and you may see something noteworthy. Some of the things to look for are:

1.   How do they appear to feel?
     Opening lines:   "You look sad" or "happy" or "angry" or "excited" or "bored".

2.   How are they dressed?
     Opening lines:   "You're dressed beautifully."
                      "Do you always dress so colorfully?"
                      "I'd never have the nerve to try to coordinate so many colors."
                      "Your shoes look so comfortable."

3.   What are they drinking?
     Opening lines:   "Is that a margarita?"
                      "I like daiquiris, too."
                      "I always feel dumb ordering Perrier."

4. What physical features stand out?
   Opening lines: "Your hair is so long."
   "Your eyes are lovely."
   "My, but you're tall."

Situations provide grand opportunities for opening lines.

"That woman you were talking to seemed stuck-up."
"I think the music's too loud."
"This place is too cold."
"I enjoyed the sermon."
"Do you know the name of this group?"
"Do these meetings happen every week?"
"Are there ever any shark attacks on this beach?"
"Does your dog always have this much energy?"
"Will this line ever start moving again?"

Talking about yourself also works well.

"I hate singles bars."
"I'm sure glad this is Friday."
"I hope I don't get sunburned."

Offering to help someone is also a great way to make contact. Whenever you see an attractive person of the opposite sex who needs help, volunteer your services. For example, if someone in a store has a quizzical look, offer to help. Do the same when you see somone overburdened with packages or trying to open a door. This advice applies as much to women as men. There's no reason why they can't help men carry packages, wash cars, etc.

## OPENING LINES THAT WORK

Corny lines

Dumb lines

Clever lines

Outlandish lines

Silly lines

Arrogant lines

Humble lines

Funny lines

Original lines

Honest, sincere lines

Lies

## OPENING LINES THAT DON'T WORK

### THE NERVOUS WRECK
As a general rule, self-confidence is an attractive quality to both sexes. Ideally you approach each new person with a demeanor that suggests that you know that you're attractive. Does that mean that you shouldn't initiate contact if you have low self-esteem? Fortunately, the answer is no. Many men and women actually prefer the self-conscious type. Others who are more attracted to the self-confident still will admire your courage in approaching them, particularly if you're a bit tongue-tied. Many will also appreciate your vulnerability. Showing your weaknesses, fears, and imperfections can be endearing to many people. They get sick of all the phonies who swagger and pretend to have their act together. An unpretentious, genuine person may be a refreshing change of pace from all the suave, sophisticated, conceited smoothies.

### SUPERFICIAL CONTACT
Many singles looking for real contact are afraid of getting involved in meaningless chatter. They deride the futility of meeting people at parties, dances, singles groups, and bars since "everyone is so phony" and "nothing significant is ever said."

If you share this attitude, you may have unrealistic expectations. Of course, initial contact between strangers is likely to be superficial. Do you expect people to spill their guts out to you in the first four minutes? Good rapport and stimulating conversation take time to develop. Don't expect people to immediately discover what excites you or makes you laugh. If you find small talk to be boring or distasteful, look upon it as paying your dues. Non-memorable conversations are the price you pay for meeting people. Your alternative is to avoid contact with strangers and risk never meeting that special person you desire.

# OVERCOMING THE FEAR
# OF REJECTION

Knowing how to initiate contact isn't enough. You have to do it. What holds most people back is an almost universal fear—the fear of rejection.

**EXERCISE**
1. Write down all the physical characteristics (face, hair, body, clothes) that might cause rejection.
2. List all the personality traits that might cause rejection.
3. Write down reasons for being rejected that have nothing to do with you (e.g., the other person is afraid of you or feels ill).

One evening I asked a group of singles to do this exercise. Their reasons follow.

**PHYSICAL REASONS FOR REJECTION**

Hair:    too short/too long
         too straight/curly
         too dark/light
Skin:    too wrinkled/not enough character lines
Nose:    too long/short
         overly broad/narrow
Lips:    too thick/thin
Neck:    too long/short
         too fat/scrawny
Head:    overly large/small

```
Body:     too tall/short
          too fat/skinny
          too old/young
          too muscle-bound/flabby
Clothes:  overly formal/casual
          too expensive/cheap
          too tight/baggy
          too colorful/drab
          too avante-garde/old-fashioned
          overly sexy/conservative
```

Needless to say, the list of physical reasons for rejection could be endless. We could continue with arms, hands, legs, chest, waist, hips, feet, etc.

## PERSONALITY TRAITS THAT CAUSE REJECTION

overtalkative/too silent      too loud/soft
laughs too much/too little      too aggressive/passive
overeducated/undereducated      too outgoing/shy
too controlled/uninhibited      overly blunt/phony
overly conventional/unconventional      too serious/relaxed
too predictable/unpredictable      too intelligent/dumb
too liberal/conservative      too common/weird
overly scrupulous/unscrupulous      too religious/irreligious
overly assertive/unassertive      too proud/humble
drinks too much/too little      too strong/weak

Again the list could be endless. You might even be rejected by two people with opposite reasons: one for being too fat, another for being too skinny. One person might find you to be too friendly, another might think you're unfriendly. As Rick Nelson sings in *Garden Party*, "you can't please everyone, so you got to please yourself."

Sometimes you are rejected for reasons that have nothing to do with you. People may be unfriendly because they are:

- ill
- in a bad mood
- depressed
- angry
- sleepy

- homosexual
- disappointed in the opposite sex
- married
- going steady
- from out of town
- too busy

Fear can also cause rejection. People may be afraid of:

- sex
- pregnancy
- venereal disease
- hepatitis
- losing their virginity
- what their friends or relatives will think
- that *you* will reject them later.

It would be great if we could dismiss rejection by saying, "It's their hangup, not mine." Unfortunately, we tend to take rejection personally. We interpret it to mean that there is something wrong with us, not them.

How, then, do you learn to get over the fear of rejection? I like to tease audiences by promising them the secret to overcoming this fear. They are always disappointed by my "magical solution": go out and get rejected. Psychologists will tell you that the best way to overcome any fear is to confront it head-on. The more you experience that which you fear, the less emotional charge it will hold for you.

I can remember the fear I experienced the first time I approached someone for a date. I was extremely scared. Sherry was a student I met in the hall as I was coming out of a classroom one day. Her class was scheduled for the next hour. Every day thereafter we bumped into each other in the hall and flirted. It was very obvious that we found each other attractive, but neither of us was willing to make the first move and risk rejection.

One day at home I analyzed the situation and concluded that there probably was a 99% chance that Sherry would say yes if I asked her out. I decided that since there was such a tiny chance of rejection I would risk it the next day. Two weeks later I finally found the courage to pop the question. She said yes.

Since that time, I've been rejected many times. I'm still afraid of being turned down, but it's no longer a traumatic experience. I've learned that life goes on after rejection.

If you're afraid of rejection, it's for good reason—rejection does hurt. But if you're paralyzed by fear like I was, chances are you need to have more experience with rejection. Otherwise you will have to spend the rest of your life depending on luck: someone special must initiate contact with you.

If you find that your fear of rejection is so great that you don't have the courage to initiate contact, you may wish to read *Thoughts and Feelings*, by Matthew McKay, Martha Davis, and Patrick Fanning. Below are brief excerpts which deal with relaxation and visualization, two skills that are crucial for overcoming the fear of rejection.

### LEARNING TO RELAX

"It is impossible to be relaxed physically and tense emotionally at the same time. You can learn to take advantage of this direct physiological link between your body and your mind. In four days of doing three practice sessions a day, you can learn to relax your muscles at will. This ability to relax will then be used to desensitize you to your fears later.

"Progressive relaxation can be practiced lying down or sitting in a chair that supports your head. You can read the instructions that follow, then close your eyes and do the exercises. It is a great help to tape record the instructions, repeating them into the machine several times so that you can play the tape and put all your concentration on relaxing."

### ABBREVIATED RELAXATION SEQUENCE

"Tense each muscle group from five to seven seconds, and then relax from 20 to 30 seconds:
1. Tense your fists, forearms, and biceps in a Charles Atlas pose; relax.
2. Wrinkle up all the muscles in your face like a walnut, and roll your head around in a circle to loosen your neck; relax.
3. Take two deep breaths, one into your chest and one

into your stomach; hold and relax.
4. Tense legs twice, one with toes pulled back and once with toes curled down; relax.

"Breathing deeply is a major key to relaxation. Between each exercise, take deep breaths into your stomach. Repeat to yourself words such as 'relax. . .calm. . .letting go' while you are breathing. Whenever tension occurs. . .take a deep breath and say to yourself, 'Relax'. The more you practice Progressive Relaxation, the deeper your relaxation will be."

Once you have learned to relax, you are ready to conquer your fear of rejection by creating a Rejection Hierarchy.

## EXERCISE
1. Make a list of 10 places where you would like to be able to initiate contact (e.g., in a bar, on the beach, at work).
2. Rearrange your list of 10 places according to your fear of rejection, so that the first on your list is the most comfortable and the last is the scariest.
3. Give your last scene a rating of five and your first scene a rating of fifty. These ratings are called "suds" which stands for subjective units of distress. Total relaxation would be zero suds. An example of a completed hierarchy would be:

| ITEM | SCENE | SUDS |
|---|---|---|
| 1 | At work | 5 |
| 2 | At a small party | 10 |
| 3 | At a large party | 15 |
| 4 | On the tennis court | 20 |
| 5 | At a dance | 25 |
| 6 | At a meeting | 30 |
| 7 | At a laundromat | 35 |
| 8 | At a singles bar | 40 |
| 9 | At a supermarket | 45 |
| 10 | On the street | 50 |

## SYSTEMATIC VISUALIZATION OF THREATENING SCENES

This technique, also from *Thoughts and Feelings*, "is based on the simple fact that lowering your anxiety reaction to the weakest item on your hierarchy lowers your reaction to all the other items to the same degree. It's a process as natural and simple as easing into a tub of hot bathwater—by the time you get all the way in, you're used to the heat and can take it with no discomfort at all.

"Get into a comfortable position where you won't be disturbed for the next 15 minutes. Have your hierarchy handy and follow these simple steps:

1.  Sitting or lying with your eyes closed, use your relaxation skills to progressively relax all the muscles in your body. . . .Let relaxation flood your body.

2.  When you are totally relaxed, allow the first scene on your hierarchy to enter your mind. Visualize the scene for five to ten seconds, making it as real as possible for yourself. Some scenes will take longer to visualize (such as imagining being at a large party). Use all your senses to create the scene, including awareness of color, touch, sound and smell. (Visualize all the people in your scene.)

3.  Notice any tension resulting from the scene and assign it a "suds" value in your mind.

4.  Staying in the scene, take a deep breath, hold it for a count of three and release it slowly. Say to yourself, 'I am relaxing. . .tension is draining away. . .I am now relaxed.' Or you can use simpler phrases such as 'relax . . .calm. . .letting go.'

5.  Notice how much your level of tension has decreased, then switch off the scene. If you want, you can end the scene by visualizing a specially relaxing place that is associated in your mind with peace and safety.

6.  Repeat this series of steps with the same scene, noticing how much your anxiety level decreases in suds each time.

7.  When twice in a row you no longer experience any anxiety, go on to the next scene in your hierarchy.

"It generally takes three or four visualizations of a scene to bring your response to it down to zero. Your first session should be about 15 minutes long and will probably handle the first three or four items on your hierarchy.

"As you gain skill and speed in relaxation and visualization, you can lengthen the sessions to thirty minutes. Stop any session if you're getting tired, bored or overly upset. You can do sessions every other day, daily, or even twice a day— the only limiting factor is fatigue.

"As you go through your hierarchy, you will notice that your ability to cope with the real life situations in that area improves. When you encounter similar situations in real life, notice any tension and use it as a cue to relax: breathe deeply and repeat your calming statements to yourself."

Overcoming the fear of rejection may not be easy, but going through life without getting your needs met is an even harder road to travel.

## HOW TO GET PEOPLE TO REJECT YOU

Rejection frequently occurs despite our best efforts. Unfortunately, some people almost seem to go out of their way to get rejected. One way to turn people off is to take the attitude, "I'm going to show you the ugly side of me right off so I can find out whether or not there's any chance of a good relationship." This policy is as bad as only putting your best foot forward and hiding everything negative. The ideal is to try to make a good impression without being phony.

Another way to get rejected is to talk constantly about ex-spouses or ex-lovers. Use some discretion. Some people will really get into your sad stories of failed relationships. Others will respond by turning off to you. There are several reasons for this:

1. They think you're still in love with your ex and are, therefore, not ready for a new relationship.
2. They think you have so much resentment towards your ex that it will spill over to them also.
3. They find your sour grapes story to be depressing and/or boring.
4. They see you as a loser who is incapable of holding on to a relationship.

It's important to be open about past relationships, but not to the point of preventing a new one. If you find that a person is engrossed in your tale of woe, then by all means give all the gory details. Otherwise reveal parts of you besides the bitter, depressed and cynical.

## MINIMIZING THE CHANCES OF REJECTION

Ideally you would totally eliminate your fear of rejection and make contact with every attractive person you see. Unfortunately, you are unlikely to ever reach that point. Since you probably only have a limited tolerance for rejection, it is crucial to choose wisely from the opportunities that come your way. Take the following precautions:

1.     Make eye contact before approaching people. That way at least you won't be a total stranger.

2.     Notice their reaction to you from afar. If they quickly turn away or frown, the chances of rejection are great.

3.     Watch your timing. For example, don't ask for a dance:
  ● when the song is almost over.
  ● after someone has been dancing strenuously.
  ● if you're a man at a disco and the band is playing a slow song. Women at discos are afraid of "perverts grinding into me" during slow numbers.
  ● if someone just lit a cigarette or ordered a drink.
  Also, don't wait to initiate contact just as people are preparing to leave. The sooner you make your move, the more time you will have to make a good impression.

## ONE NIGHT STANDS

A major problem for large numbers of singles, particularly women, is how to deal with one night stands. It's natural to feel disappointed if you meet someone nice, get involved physically, and then never hear from them again. Your self-esteem will likely go down as a result of this "rejection". It's important to realize that one night stands don't necessarily mean that you're less of a person or unattractive. Your lover(s) have simply chosen not to get involved with you again. Some of the more common reasons for this are:

1.   They already are in a steady relationship or are married. Perhaps they concealed this fact from you for fear that it would make you less attracted to them. Instead of exposing themselves to your hostility by letting you know, they prefer to drop you quietly.

2.   They didn't enjoy themselves. Just because you enjoyed the sexual encounter doesn't mean they did, despite what they may say. They may not have achieved orgasm. You may not be their type sexually. It's possible for two people to find each other attractive and still be incompatible in bed.

3.   They find you to be very attractive and are afraid of falling for you. Many single people have a fear of intimacy and committed relationships. You may be part of a long string of one night stands, so don't take it personally.

4.   They could be "notch on the belt artists". Some singles, particularly men, need to prove their value through sexual conquests. Once you have been seduced, you lose your value to them so they move on to the next challenge.

5.   They may be afraid to call and ask for another date for fear of being rejected. They may think that you didn't enjoy yourself with them and are unlikely to want a repeat performance.

6.   They may be waiting for *you* to call *them*.

When lovers fail to call after a first encounter, you can do one of two things: you can speculate on why they have rejected you or you can call and ask point blank why they haven't pursued another encounter with you. Hopefully, they'll be honest and share why they haven't called. You may even clear up a misunderstanding. For example, Frank is a 35 year old designer. "When I first met Susie, we really clicked. Going to bed with her was a cinch. The only problem was that a couple of times that night, she casually mentioned a fiance. I figured that I didn't have a chance for a steady relationship so I never called again. Fortunately, Susie called me and told me how hurt she was that I hadn't called. When I explained the reason, she burst out laughing. She explained that the guy was her ex-fiance. They had only broken up a couple of weeks earlier, so she still habitually referred to him as her fiance. After we cleared things up, we resumed dating. We wound up going down the altar together."

## GOODBYE WITHOUT RESENTMENT

It's easy to get angry when someone rejects you and say, "I don't have to put up with this; if people don't want me, I can go it alone." Unfortunately, this attitude won't get your needs met. It's foolish to expect everyone to find you attractive. They have the same right you have to set whatever romantic standards they wish.

## EXERCISE

Write down all the people you have rejected in the past week. This includes all the times that:

- you turned away from an unattractive person making eye contact with you.
- you excused yourself from a conversation with someone unattractive.
- you refused a date.

Hopefully, your list will be as long (or longer) than that of those who have rejected you. Rejection protects both you and them from undesirable relationships.

## HOW TO REJECT SOMEONE

Rejecting someone can be more painful than getting rejected. You may feel guilty saying no to someone who initiates contact. It must be done, however, if you are to clear the tracks for someone new. Instead of wasting time with the wrong person, you could be meeting someone right for you.

How do you say no to someone who approaches you? The best way is to say, "No, thank you." You're thanking people for the compliment they paid you by initiating contact, but declining the opportunity to chat, dance, have a drink, or date them. You don't have to invent excuses, apologies, or explanations. You have a right to refuse contact with anyone without justifying your decision. You're not responsible for their hurt feelings—they knew they were risking rejection when they approached you.

There are many ways that making excuses can backfire. For example, suppose you are asked to dance. If you lie and say, "No, my feet hurt," they may insist on sitting at your table instead. They're only taking you at your word that you're not rejecting them but the dancing option. Now you have the problem of getting rid of them. In the same situation, if you reply, "No, I don't like this song," you may be off the hook. On the other hand, if they ask you later for a dance, you're going to be stuck with saying yes or rejecting them again.

Another example is someone unattractive asking you for a date for Saturday night. If you say, "No, I already have a date that night," hopefully they'll move on. However, if they persist and present alternative times, you are probably going to feel forced to break down and say yes or make it obvious that you just aren't attracted to them. In the same situation, you can say, "No, I already have a boyfriend/girlfriend." This is the champion dodge. It usually works, but only if you aren't going to see them again.

You probably will feel better about yourself if you are truthful in these situations. Many of the people you are rejecting will appreciate your honesty. They will be thinking, "thanks for not b.s.ing me" whether they say so or not.

If people you reject foolishly demand an explanation, they are choosing to open themselves to being hurt. You may lie to spare their feelings or choose to be blunt and say you find them unattractive. Since *they* asked *you*, they are responsible for being hurt, not you.

## A FINAL NOTE ON REJECTION

Franklin Delano Roosevelt was once asked for the secret for overcoming the fear of rejection. His reply was, "I realize that other people are just as afraid to speak to me —especially the first time—as I am to speak to them."

71

# THE ART OF CONVERSATION

Being able to initiate contact is of little use unless you also know how to survive the first four minutes of contact with strangers. According to Leonard Zunin, in his book, *Contact: The First Four Minutes*, this is the average amount of time you have to convince others that they should get to know you better. It's vital, therefore, to learn the art of conversation. This involves mastery of two apparently easy skills: talking and listening. Unfortunately, many of us find difficulty with one or the other. Two types of mismatches frequently result: two poor talkers get together and have a very dull conversation or two poor listeners converse and wind up fighting for the attention of the other. Even if a good talker meets a good listener, problems eventually arise. The good talker resents having to do all the talking in order to keep the conversation going. The good listener becomes bored with the same old stories, thoughts and feelings.

## PEOPLE DON'T UNDERSTAND ME

A common problem of poor talkers is that they are difficult to understand. Shari is a 25 year old letter carrier for the post office. "I've always been extremely shy and quiet. My teachers tried to push me into giving oral reports and participating in discussions, but I was reluctant. I'm fairly attractive so guys come up to me occasionally, but I have difficulty sustaining a conversation with them. It's embarrassing for me to watch them straining to hear. I know they feel uncomfortable constantly asking me to repeat

73

myself. Eventually they give up and just pretend to be listening. They lose interest and walk away. It's very discouraging."

One solution to this problem is to go somewhere private and practice talking at the top of your lungs, like the legendary Greek orator, Demosthenes. Later ask a person you trust to listen while you shout. Practice talking louder to other friends and finally to strangers. Ask them to remind you to speak up each time your voice begins to fade. A second solution is to use the exercise on page 65 and substitute your fear of conversing with strangers. A third solution is to see a therapist.

## NOTHING TO SAY

A common complaint of poor talkers is that they have nothing to say. Rob is a 32 year old construction worker. "I know this sounds stupid, but I really have nothing to say. I'd much rather listen to people who are smart and have lots of things to talk about."

If you are silent most of the time, you probably defend yourself with the same excuse. Claiming that you have nothing to say is really a lie you tell yourself to cover up your fears. In reality, you have an unlimited number of interesting topics at your disposal. A good place to begin is with yourself. That's the most fascinating topic you have to discuss. You are the world's foremost expert on the subject and have numerous interesting things to reveal. As Arthur Wassmer points out in *Making Contact*, "Remember, what may seem an everyday experience to you can strike a listener as fascinating; it happens more often than you think."

**EXERCISE**

1.  In order to discover the interesting person you are, write a factual autobiography of 1000 words. Don't worry about grammar, spelling, or handwriting (as long as you can read your own writing). Include all the basic facts such as:

    • where and when you were born
    • where you went to school and what classes you took
    • where you worked and what your responsibilities were

- who your friends were and what they were like
- what your parents and relatives were like
- different homes, towns and countries where you have lived

2. Now add facts about your emotional life. How did you feel in particular homes, schools, jobs, situations, etc? How did you feel towards your parents, relatives and friends and how did you relate to them? List as many emotions as possible to flesh out your factual auto-biography. Be as specific as possible. Don't write, "I felt good." Mention specific emotions such as love, hate, joy, sadness, depression, anxiety, excitement, ecstasy, jealousy, hope and despair.

3. Now add funny stories that happened to you person-ally or that you witnessed.

Your autobiography will give you a wealth of stories to relate to people you meet. There are numerous other areas that provide conversational ammunition:

1. What happened to you five minutes ago, yesterday, or last week.

2. Your job or classes you're taking. Be careful, however, not to fall into the trap of always talking shop. If you are obsessed by school or work, you may bore every-one with tedious recitals of everything that happened to you in the classroom or on the job.

3. The weather. Even though it's considered trite, the weather is really an interesting subject. It's also one of the easiest to discuss with most anyone.

4. Some book you've just read (or magazine or newspaper article).

5. Current events (local, national and international).

6. Sports.

7. Religion, sex and politics. These are all-time favorite topics. Granted, they are supposed to be taboo and can be risky. Some people will be intolerant if you have different views from theirs. Certainly there is a risk of getting into a nasty argument and having a promising relationship collapse. However, if you do get seriously involved, your opinions on these subjects invariably are revealed. Better to nip a doomed relationship in the bud than discover too late that you clash on too many subjects to be compatible.

8. A joke or funny story about yourself, a friend, or someone you read or heard about. Don't be afraid to tell a story that makes you appear foolish. You will endear yourself to others if you show that you can laugh and make fun of yourself.

9. A recent trip. People love to hear about exotic places like Hawaii, Bali, Hong Kong, and Rome. Don't be afraid to talk about trips to less impressive places or towns close to home. As long as *you* are turned on to the subject, you have the potential for stimulating your listeners. Frequently people will share their own experiences traveling to the same or similar places.

10. Some task you have undertaken (painting the kitchen, fixing your car, writing a resume).

11. Your hobbies (e.g., stamp-collecting, needlepoint, building military models).

12. The other person. People love to hear you talk about them, as long as you aren't overly negative or critical.

13. Your hopes and fears.

14. Your dreams (no matter how wild or unrealistic they may be). Ask people to help interpret the symbolism in your dreams or if they've had similar ones. If your dreams are x-rated, be careful to choose an appropriate audience.

15. Your feelings at the moment. People usually feel privileged if you open up and share what's going on inside of you.

16. Something you don't like about them. Ask them for permission first, unless you're sure they won't be offended. Be gentle and constructive.

17. Your problem of being a poor talker. Once you've established that you have a problem, you will feel less self-conscious about it. The odds are the other person will be sympathetic and encourage you to talk. You'll probably feel less pressure to be entertaining.

18. How much you like or love them. This is often the most difficult subject to discuss, but it's usually the most appreciated.

You don't always have to be witty and fascinating when talking about yourself. As Arthur Wassmer points out: "People are not interested in you for your entertainment value. They can get better entertainment than most of us can provide simply by turning on the television. It is *you* that they are interested in and contact that they seek."

## FINDING SOMETHING IN COMMON

A key to successful conversation is talking about something you have in common with the other person. No matter how different they may appear, you have many things in common with all human beings. The trick is to discover what these things are. Here are only a few possibilities:

1. born in the same town or city
2. vacationed at the same places
3. went to the same school, college or university
4. studied the same subjects
5. read the same books
6. worked at the same job or for the same company
7. have the same hobbies
8. play the same games or sports
9. belong to the same church, club or political party

10. have similar dreams, fantasies, plans or ambitions
11. had the same joys or problems with parents, relatives, friends or lovers.
12. know the same people
13. admire the same musicians, entertainers, movie and television stars, politicians, athletes, sports teams, artists, philosophers, psychologists, etc.
14. have children of similar ages.

When you meet someone new, just listen closely to clues as to what you might have in common and you'll soon be off to the races.

### WHAT IF I'M BORING?

Diane is a 40 year old divorced homemaker. She's a loving mother of three and is always watching the kids, cleaning house, doing errands, or watching television. "I get the impression that nobody wants to listen to me except my children. When I meet people, they're always fidgeting and avoiding eye contact. They seldom want to stay around and talk. I guess I must be very boring."

The easiest way to develop stimulating subject matter is to lead a more interesting life. If you're a homebody, perhaps all you need is to get out of the house more often. If you spend too much time with your children, try to converse more often with adults. Possibly you're in a rut and need to watch less television, listen to fewer records, or read fewer romance novels. Taking a job or signing up for a class may add spice to your life. Going to a museum, attending an art exhibit, or joining a club or organization might lead to more stimulating discussion topics. Going on a trip will add many interesting stories to your conversations. Try something new and exciting.

A second solution is to read more. The latest best-sellers are excellent conversation topics. Newspapers and magazines also provide interesting subjects for discussion.

A third solution is to go to movies, operas, symphonies and other entertainment and cultural events. You'll be able to discuss them with others who do likewise.

A fourth possibility is to avoid the following pitfalls in conversations: 1) talking too much about the past ("in the good old days. . ."); 2) complaining all the time; 3) constantly talking behind people's backs.

A fifth solution is to rehearse. Some people have great memories. Others can't tell a joke without forgetting the punch line or can't repeat something they've heard or read without getting their facts all mixed up. If you have this problem, practice telling jokes, stories, facts and interesting ideas. Don't memorize word-for-word, but practice enough times so you won't make a fool of yourself (or fear that you'll make a fool of yourself).

## USING A TAPE RECORDER

Listening to yourself on a tape recorder during a conversation can provide valuable insights. Possibly the content of your conversations is interesting but your delivery is dull. Speaking too slowly, for example, can drive your listeners crazy. If that's your problem use the tape recorder to practice conversing when you are alone. Concentrate on speaking as rapidly as possible.

If you speak in a monotone, again practice on the tape recorder. Try to put enthusiasm in your voice. Talk in front of a mirror and practice increasing your use of facial expressions and gestures.

Another problem is the overfrequent use of certain phrases such as "you know," "basically," "uh," etc. Practice speaking about the same topic over and over until you eliminate the repetitive phrase(s).

## HOW TO GET PEOPLE TO LISTEN

Be sensitive to whether or not people are listening to you. If you notice that your "listeners" are staring at you with a blank expression, avoiding eye contact, or are unusually silent, the odds are that they're not really listening and you're wasting your time. You're also boring them, which decreases the chance that they will want to spend time with you again. What can you do with an inattentive listener?

1.    Change the subject. There are an infinite number of other topics to discuss. If you can't think of anything stimulating, ask them if there's anything they would like to discuss. Possibly they've been patiently waiting for you to finish before bringing up something else that's important to them.

2.   Ask them a question about what you've been saying. You'll jar them into paying closer attention in the future.

3.   Raise your voice. Possibly they're having a difficult time hearing you.

4.   Touch them gently.

5.   Ask, "Am I boring you?" Say it in a gentle or humorous way so that they don't take offense or feel threatened.

If worse comes to worse, terminate the conversation. Better to quit while you're ahead (or only a little behind) than to vainly attempt to prolong a lackluster conversation. There are many reasons why a person may not be in the mood to converse with you:

1.   They feel physically ill, fatigued or sleepy.
2.   They're in a bad mood.
3.   They're distracted by a personal problem.
4.   They need to do something else, like use the restroom, get another drink or make a telephone call.
5.   They're late for another commitment.
6.   They want to talk to someone else in the room.

If you master the skills in this chapter, you'll be halfway towards your goal of being a good conversationalist. The next chapter deals with the second half, which is often harder: becoming a good listener.

# BECOMING A GOOD LISTENER

Are you a good listener? Don't confuse hearing with listening, which are really two different skills. If what you hear goes in one ear and out the other, forming a loving relationship will be extremely difficult.

**EXERCISE**
List your closest friends, relatives and business associates. Rank them on a scale of 1 to 10, 1 meaning completely boring and 10 meaning always fascinating.

If you find that you've labeled the majority as boring, you probably have one of two problems: 1) you're socializing or working with the wrong people, or 2) you're a poor listener. The likelihood is the latter. Bored listeners usually don't listen at all. If they ever stopped and really listened, they might actually enjoy themselves. A good example is Ed, a 49 year old computer software salesman. "I used to always find people boring. I'd meet all kinds of women— I had a very active social life and am very outgoing. Some of the women were attractive physically and I'd get involved, but eventually the relationships would fizzle out. I'd always get tired of them and move on to someone new.

"Everyone thought I was just a playboy—afraid of love and intimacy. I kept arguing that if I ever met the right women—someone who was interesting, funny, intelligent, *and* pretty—that I'd go for her. Unfortunately, all the interesting women were physically unattractive and all the cute ones seemed to be empty-headed.

"One day I read an article on how to listen effectively. After practicing some of the suggestions, I was amazed by the results. All of a sudden, almost everybody became interesting. Every time I felt bored, restless, or uneasy, I used one of the listening techniques in the article and presto! I was interested again.

"Gradually the truth hit me. The reason I found most conversations boring was because the only person I ever really listened to was myself! Sure, I'm intelligent, educated, witty, and articulate. Others seem to enjoy listening to me, but I bore myself. I've already heard my thoughts, feelings, jokes and stories a million times. Once I started listening to others, I stopped shying away from meeting new people for fear that they'd bore me.

"Another interesting result is that people seem to be listening more closely to me. I guess they used to turn me off because I'd done the same to them."

What if you're the opposite: someone who is quiet, shy and seldom contributes much to a conversation. At least you're a good listener, right? Wrong! Shy people are not only poor talkers; they're usually poor listeners. If you're shy, you probably feel uncomfortable in conversations, particularly with strangers. Your fears and discomfort can distract you from others and what they're saying. You need to learn to relax (which is discussed in detail in the chapter on rejection) when you converse. Every time you feel tense, nervous or uncomfortable in a conversation, you should take a deep breath so you can relax and listen. Surprisingly, the same advice holds true for people like Ed who aren't shy but constantly feel bored during conversations. You get nervous and restless when you're bored. Relaxing will enable you to listen attentively and become interested in what other people are saying.

Becoming a good listener is one of the most useful qualities you can develop in your search for a romantic partner. If you're a good listener, you have a tremendous advantage over possible rivals. When you listen attentively, you are accomplishing several things:

1. You're complimenting people. They will feel that you value them and what they have to say.
2. You're encouraging them to open themselves and

share their thoughts and feelings.

3.    You're increasing the chances that they will continue conversing with you.

**EXERCISE**

If you suspect you're a poor listener, check it out with your friends and relatives. Ask them to be specific about how you might be a poor listener. Assure them that you will listen in silence to what they have to say and won't interrupt them. Only after they finish should you ask follow-up questions. Resist the temptation to defend yourself. Thank them for giving you honest, constructive criticism, no matter how much it hurts.

Listed below are eight types of poor listeners. See if any sound familiar.

1.    The motor mouths. They never seem to stop talking. It's almost impossible to get a word in edgewise. If you're a motor mouth, practice being completely silent while others talk.

2.    The plan-aheaders. They don't listen because they're continuously planning what they're going to say next, after someone makes the mistake of pausing for breath. If you're a plan-aheader, try to drop your own thoughts and concentrate solely on those of the other person.

3.    The interrupters. They can't wait their turn, so they interrupt your train of thought with comments or questions. If you're an interrupter, stifle yourself. Wait until people completely stop talking before adding your two cents worth.

4.    The misinterpreters. They manage to misunderstand whatever you say, no matter how clearly you express yourself. If you're a misinterpreter, practice repeating what people say. Ask them if you've been accurate. If they answer no, don't argue. Ask them to repeat their point *their* way.

5.    The egocentrics. They always turn the focus of the

83

conversation back to their favorite topic—themselves. If you're egocentric, practice omitting the use of the pronouns I, me and my. Exclusively use the pronouns you, your, he, she, him, her, his, them and their when conversing.

6. The tangent lovers. They focus on some insignificant part of what you're saying and totally overlook the important parts. If you're a tangent lover, tell people about your problem and ask them to insist on returning to their main point immediately after you digress.

7. The deaf. They have a hearing problem but are too proud to admit it. Rather than wear a hearing aid, they choose to miss out on a significant part of what people are saying. People with poor hearing often conceal this fact by being motor mouths. As long as they're doing the talking, nobody will discover that their hearing is impaired. Seniors frequently have this problem. They may be unwilling to face the reality of poor hearing because to them it's an admission that they're over the hill and useless. If you're deaf or hard of hearing, buy a hearing aid.

8. The easily offended. They are antagonized by almost anything you say. Every imagined slight is an insult. Your disagreement with anything they say makes you an enemy. Conversations with them usually end in anger and frustration. If you are easily offended, your problem is low self-esteem. Consider seeing a psychotherapist.

## TEN SINS OF POOR LISTENERS
Below are ten blocks to good listening. Examples are given on how you might employ them to prevent real contact with people you meet.

1. Comparing. With this block, you are distracted from listening by comparing your attractiveness, intelligence, education, health, etc. with others. For example, a man tells you about his new job. Rather than listen attentively to a description of his responsi-

bilities and how he feels about the job, you mentally start comparing your salary and position on the corporate ladder with his. You also speculate on whether he is as competent as you are.

2. Suspecting. Instead of trusting that others are telling you the truth, you're always looking beneath the surface for subtle clues that they're lying or concealing secrets. For example, a woman tells you about her recent divorce. Instead of giving her the benefit of the doubt and believing her description of what her husband was like and why the marriage collapsed, you try to read between the lines and fantasize about what the relationship was "really like". "I'll bet she was a constant nag" or "she was probably unfaithful" are thoughts that go through your mind. Meanwhile, you miss half of what she's telling you about what really happened.

   Certainly it's true that people sometimes lie or tell half-truths, but generally people are telling the truth. There's no need to be gullible, but the best policy is to accept what people say unless you have good reason to doubt them.

3. Filtering. This is where you only hear what you want to hear and filter out significant parts of the message people try to communicate to you. For example, someone tells you that he or she really likes your personality but isn't sexually attracted to you. The person also informs you about a steady lover and states a preference for a platonic relationship with you. You miss the part about your attractive personality and decide the person dislikes you. You refuse to have anything further to do with the person and miss out on the opportunity for a pleasant friendship.

   Another example: someone tells you that he/she thinks you are attractive but is hoping to marry someone younger. You also learn about the person's current lover. You filter out the part about the desire for someone younger and conclude that all you have to do is bide your time and wait for the other lover to leave the picture. Then you can move in, since the person admits to being attracted to you. You cling to this unrealistic fantasy instead of going on to a more likely prospect for a long-term relationship.

4. Judging. You're so busy evaluating whether people are good or bad, competent or incompetent, admirable or contemptible, that you miss a good deal of what they are saying to you. For example, a man tells you some of his sexual experiences. You learn intimate details about his love life: needs, fantasies, disappointments, joys. Meantime you're judging whether or not he is sufficiently moral or sexually liberated, too "straight" or too "perverted". A one-time opportunity for intimacy is lost.

5. Identifying. Everything people say reminds you of yourself. You switch the subject away from them to you before they have a chance to finish their story or point. For example, a man tells you about the new car he is thrilled to have bought. This immediately reminds you of a car of the same make you had ten years ago. You interrupt the man in mid-sentence and spend the next five minutes talking about your ex-car. Then you wonder why he wanders off after a perfunctory good-bye to talk to someone else.

7. Advising. Sometimes you can help people by giving them advice, but most of the time they primarily need a good listener. They can be very resentful if you don't give them the opportunity to just share their thoughts and feelings without having to justify them. For example, a woman tells you how horrible she feels after just discovering her lover is gay. You launch into a lecture about how common this is becoming and all the new support groups for women experiencing this problem. The irony is that you are actually giving her good advice, but she walks off feeling negative towards you because of your inability to just be there and listen.

8. Arguing. Many people enjoy the stimulation of a good discussion or debate. Unfortunately, most of us are

very poor listeners when we are intent on proving someone wrong. For example, a man tells you about how difficult it is for him to adjust to his recent conversion from Judaism to Catholicism. You immediately point out what a horrible mistake he made and how the Vatican "owns half of Italy". After a heated exchange, your potential new friend walks away to talk to someone else who is willing to listen to his feelings.

9. Joking. This is a way of evading unpleasant topics. Unfortunately, joking when seriousness is appropriate is only postponing the inevitable confrontation with reality. For example, a woman suggests you spend the night with her. You feel uncomfortable with this and nervously joke, "But what will the bartender think if we leave together?"

10. Changing the subject. This is another way of avoiding unpleasantry. For example, someone you find unattractive asks to see you again. You pretend you didn't hear because of the loud music and ask, "Do you want to dance again?"

## EXERCISE
1. Spend a week watching how many "sins" you commit when conversing with friends. Determine your top three blocks to good listening and spend the week concentrating on doing the opposite.

2. Spend another week watching your interaction with strangers. See if you still have a tendency to make the same three mistakes. Again spend a week doing the opposite.

## ACTIVE LISTENING
So far we've looked at listening as something passive: all you have to do is sit sphinx-like and avoid certain habits. Unfortunately, this isn't enough. In order to be effective, listening must be active. This involves five basic skills.

1. Clarifying. Frequently ask questions when you don't fully understand what someone is saying or you aren't

certain that you heard them correctly.

2. Responding. Be sure to give people feedback while they're talking. Frequently say "yeah," "uh huh," etc. to encourage them. Tell them what you think or feel about what they are saying. Try to be non-judgmental in your feedback. The best way of doing this is to make "I" statements rather than "you" statements. For example:

> Instead of saying: "*You* sure fouled that up."
> Say: "*I* think I would have done things differently."

> Instead of saying: "*You* sure are willing to put up with a lot of guff."
> Say: "*I* have no patience with people that treat me that way."

> Instead of saying: "*You* have a sick attitude toward sex."
> Say: "*I* am more liberated about sex than you."

3. Understanding. It's important to realize that people act the way they do because they believe (often incorrectly) that it's the best thing to do. You may often find yourself turning off to people because they say, feel, or do things you disdain. Try to understand why people are the way they are. Ask yourself what purpose is served by feeling or acting the way they do.

For example, you meet someone who recites a boring litany of faults about an ex-spouse. Your natural inclination is to be judgmental and say to yourself, "Who wants to listen to all this crap?" You turn off to the conversation and start daydreaming. Effective listening requires a different course. Try to understand why people are angry or hurt. If you listen closely, you'll probably learn a great deal about some very important experiences. It's unimportant whether their ex-spouses were as rotten as they would have you believe. Surely they suffered a great deal in their broken marriages and have some cause for complaint. Though the subject may be unpleasant, people are giving you the gift of seeing their inner selves. You may never again be given the chance to see other things that are more attractive if you close yourself off to their ugly sides.

4. Being open-minded. There's nothing wrong with having strong convictions ("standing up for what I believe in"). Many of us have a tendency, however, to close our ears to views that differ from our own. The secret to being open-minded is to realize that since you're human, anything you believe could be wrong—no matter how certain you are.

5. Empathizing. Try to see things from the other person's perspective, rather than your own. Put aside your own prejudices, beliefs, hopes and fears and identify with theirs. A good way to do this is to actually pretend you are that other person.

Changing your listening habits may be a chore in the beginning, but after a while, good listening becomes second nature. You will reap the following rewards for your efforts:

1. People will like you, value your company and seek you out.
2. They will open themselves up to you and share a treasure chest of their deepest thoughts, feelings and secrets.
3. People are more likely to listen when you speak.
4. You will find most people to be interesting and entertaining.
5. You will actually look forward to meeting new people and will value seeing them over and over.
6. You will feel closer to people and find it easier to form loving relationships with them.

The world is full of good talkers, but good listeners can be a treasure. Become a good listener and many people will decide that *you* are a special someone.

## HOW TO HANDLE A POOR LISTENER
What should you do if you meet someone attractive

who is a poor listener? You have three choices. The first is to change them. Changing people is seldom easy, particularly in the case of poor listeners, since they don't listen very well when you ask them to change. While it's certainly not your obligation to change them into good listeners, it's wise to take some responsibility for their behavior with you. Ask yourself three questions:

1.   Have I attempted to explain their problem to them in a calm, non-threatening manner? If you don't point out the problem, how else will they find out?

2.   Have I stood up for my rights instead of meekly submitting to their poor listening behavior?

3.   Can I honestly claim that I have not encouraged the poor listener to act that way? Frequently, victims of mistreatment bear major responsibility for their sad predicament.

If you answered no to any of these questions, you need to change your own behavior. Hopefully, the poor listener will do likewise. If you answered yes to all three questions, changing the poor listener obviously isn't the solution. You are faced with two more alternatives. One is to accept them. If you're getting enough rewards from the relationship, it may be worth sustaining. The second alternative is to drop them. A lifetime spent with a poor listener can be one of endless frustration and lack of intimacy. There are millions of good listeners out there. Find one.

# ESTABLISHING INTIMACY

Having a great conversation with someone new and attractive is exciting. The next step is arranging to see one another again. The question is where? There are several important considerations.

1.  You should go somewhere or do something that both of you will enjoy. Ideally your first date (and subsequent ones as well) will be a joint decision. There's nothing wrong with taking the initiative and asking someone out to a particular event or place, but it's usually better to discuss several options and find one the both of you will enjoy. Otherwise, the other person may agree to go along because of attraction to you rather than the activity. You will then be expected to be so stimulating and entertaining that you make up for what your date considers to be an unpleasant activity.

    When someone attractive invites you for a date, don't be afraid to be assertive if the suggestion is something you might not enjoy. Make a counter-suggestion or just say, "I'd like to see you again but that just doesn't interest me. Can we think of something else?" Otherwise you may find yourself sleeping through the last half of a symphony, having nightmares after a horror film, or shivering and suffering through the rigors of camping.

2.   Choose an activity that will enable you to get to know the other person. Going to a rock concert may be fun but it's difficult to communicate with the music blaring. Sharing a meal, a cup of coffee, or a drink may be the easiest way to carry on a sustained and intimate conversation. On the other hand, if you find it difficult to converse with new friends for more than a few minutes at a time, it might be wise to choose an event where there is less need for conversation: a play, movie or concert. You can still converse during the breaks and while driving to and from the event.

3.   If you invite your date to your home for dinner, be sure that both of you will enjoy the meal. If you're a meat and potatoes person and your date is a vegetarian, cooking a suitable meal may require some thought and discussion. Other problems may arise. Your date may be on a diet while you're trying to gain weight. Your favorite dish (liver and onions) may make others nauseated. If you plan your menu enough in advance, check with your partner ahead of time to make sure it's all right.

4.   If you are invited to your date's home for a meal be sure to spell out any unusual eating habits, such as vegetarianism, special medical diet, allergies, etc. If you're a finicky eater, you have a problem. You may be afraid of offending your host by asking what's on the menu. If you don't do so, however, you run the risk of either offending your date by barely touching your meal or offending your stomach by forcing down distasteful morsels.

5.   This advice holds true for restaurants as well. Find out what kind of food is served at the establishment and make sure both of you will enjoy it. Don't let someone surprise you by taking you to an unannounced restaurant unless you're the kind of person who'll eat most anything.

6.   Don't be afraid to do the unusual. Most dates traditionally involve dinner, dancing or a movie. There's

nothing wrong with going out to breakfast or lunch instead. You can go roller or ice skating, horseback riding, canoeing, or sailing. You can also go for a ferry boat ride or visit an amusement park, the county fair, etc.

7. Don't feel compelled to spend a lot of money unless you can afford it. Otherwise you may set overly high expectations for the date and be sorely disappointed ("I dropped a hundred bucks and didn't even get a goodnight kiss.") There is nothing wrong with doing things that are either free or only involve the expense of a short drive: walking along the beach and watching the sunset (or sunrise); going to a zoo or park; attending free lectures, exhibits, festivals and parades. The point of the date is to have a good time and get to know one another, not impress your partner with the size of your bank account.

How do you achieve intimacy in romantic relationships? There's nothing complicated. You only need to do two things: Pry and Reveal. When you pry, you ask people to open themselves so you can get to know them better; in turn you reveal yourself so they get to know you. It's as simple as that.

## PRYING
Being nosy or inquisitive is considered a "no-no" in our society. This fear of intruding on the privacy of others is a major reason for the lack of intimacy and prevalence of loneliness in this country. The way to get to know someone is to ask questions and listen attentively. What kinds of questions should you ask someone you don't know very well? There are four types.

1. Small talk questions. They break the ice and also provide important information. Where are you from? Have you been here before? What do you do? What kinds of hobbies do you have? Do you dance? What kind of music do you like? Do you have any kids? Have you ever been married?

2.  Follow-up questions. The beauty of small talk questions is that usually you gain more information than you expected. You are then in a position to ask follow-up questions. You can ask them to clarify or elaborate on what they told you without appearing nosy (after all, they brought up the subject themselves.) Suppose you ask a man what he does for a living (small talk question) and he answers that he's "a police officer, unfortunately." Now you have the opportunity to ask the perfect follow-up question, "Why do you say unfortunately?" You're likely to learn a great deal about this man: all the stresses, fears, challenges, frustrations and thrills that go with being a policeman. Your follow-up questions won't be interpreted as your being overly-curious because he opened the door himself by mentioning that he found his occupation to be unfortunate.

    Another example: you ask an attractive woman at a disco, "Have you ever been here before?" (small talk question). She replies, "I've only been here once but I wish I could come more often." This presents you with the opportunity to ask, "Why don't you come more often?" (follow-up question) You're likely to find out a great deal of personal information by pursuing this tack. You may discover that she doesn't come more often because she works very hard and is exhausted when she gets home. Perhaps she has an invalid parent at home.

3.  Opinion questions. These can be a little more personal. You're asking people to take a stand and risk offending you or incurring your disapproval. Who should I vote for? Is there a God? Where are the best investments? What do you think about marijuana? Do you believe in dating someone of a different race?

    People have opinions about most everything, so there's no limit to the number of opinion questions you can ask. The more controversial the question, of course, the greater the risk that the two of you will disagree. If you're the kind of person who is close-minded and intolerant of the views of others, it might be wise for you to limit yourself to questions in areas where you don't have strong opinions. As long as you don't try to prove that people are wrong, stupid, ignorant, or immoral, the likelihood is that they will enjoy sharing their opinions with you.

4.    Personal questions. These provide information that is usually kept private. Are you a virgin? Do you have a drinking problem? Do you ever fantasize about rape? Do you get along well with your children? Are you happy? Are you looking for love or just a one night stand? How do you feel about my smoking? Do you find me attractive? Am I your type? Are you feeling uptight talking to me right now? Are you self-conscious about your weight? Are you afraid of dying? Are you afraid that you're too old to remarry?

Personal questions such as these may take courage to ask—and answer—but the information they provide is the fuel for intimacy. If you don't ask them, you will be safe from both the hazards and the joys of being close to others.

Sometimes you may be lucky and run into attractive people who are naturally open. You don't have to pry because their lives "are an open book". These people are very rare. Even extremely open people often need some prodding. They aren't going to spill their guts unless they feel confident that you are open and interested in learning about them. When you ask personal questions, you are likely to receive one of the following responses:

- They answer fully and honestly. Ideally people will choose this option and you are well on your way to intimacy.
- They don't answer because they didn't hear you or misunderstood your question. Be cognizant of this possibility. Don't be afraid to repeat the question loudly or in different words if you suspect they misheard or misunderstood you.
- They don't answer because they feel uncomfortable with the question right now. They may feel more comfortable later. If you suspect this might be the case, give them another chance later after they've

gotten to know you better. Timing is often crucial. A too-personal question at the start of a conversation may be quite comfortable ten minutes later.

- They don't answer because they think you're an inquisitive busybody who has no right to ask. If you see this in their eyes, tell them, "You probably think I'm a nosy boor for asking this, but I would really like to get to know you better." If they don't react positively, chances are you're flirting with someone with whom you will have difficulty achieving intimacy. Choose someone else.
- They answer, but not completely. Gently ask a follow-up question. If they still don't answer completely, save the question for later.
- They answer, but dishonestly. If you suspect this is the case, say in a pleasant, lighthearted way, "I'm sorry for putting you on the spot, but I'd like to get to know you better. Feel free to lie or refuse to answer anything I ask you." They may laugh and give you the honest answer then and there or at least plan to do so later if they find they like you.

Asking questions, particularly personal ones, can be scary. Fortunately, as the possibility of rejection increases, so does the chance for intimacy. If you have a delicate ego, take the following precautions:

1.  Avoid personal questions until after you've developed strong rapport.

2.  Slowly escalate the heaviness of your inquiries. Ask slightly personal questions first and then move on to more intimate ones.

3.  Preemptively withdraw a personal question before they answer if you can see worry or anger sweep suddenly over their faces. Make a hasty retreat by saying, "I really shouldn't be asking you something this personal—you might put me on the spot in return." This is a pleasant, joking way of relieving the tension and enabling them to avoid questions with which they feel uncomfortable.

Humor is the most effective tool for prying. If you can sugar-coat even the most intimate inquiry with humor, you are likely to get full and honest answers. If a person appears reluctant to answer your personal questions, you can joke, "If I wasn't so chicken, I'd ask you _____" Another way of asking is, "Please don't hit me if I ask you _____"

## MAKING PEOPLE TALK

The most vital ingredient for intimacy is trust. Someone who trusts you is unlikely to be closed. In order to open up, people must feel confident that:

1. You won't spill their secrets to others without specific permission. If you're a blabbermouth, very few people will be foolish enough to share personal information or secrets with you. It's vital to develop a reputation for confidentiality. Always keep a secret, no matter how juicy the story or how much someone pleads with you to share it. Be sure you are clear as to what information you are expected to keep confidential. This prevents future arguments and recriminations.

2. You won't use the information against them later. The more people tell you about themselves, the more ammunition they're giving you to use against them. They make themselves vulnerable each time they reveal a weak spot. Resist the temptation to use this information against them in the heat of anger or for temporary advantage. Every time you do this, they will feel betrayed and be less likely to confide in you again. Intimacy in a relationship cannot be maintained if a person suspects you will use their revelations unscrupulously.

3. You won't be judmental or critical. There's nothing wrong with letting someone know that you have different moral standards or points of view. You may reveal that in similar circumstances, you might have acted differently, as long as you make it clear they are not obligated to be like you.

4.    You won't reject them. Once people learn that rela-
      tionships with you are conditional on their acting in
      certain ways, they will take care not to let you see
      other sides of them. Hanging up the phone, leaving
      them in disgust, or acting cold or silent after they
      share something about themselves are the prescription
      for zero intimacy in a relationship.

      People are likely to tell you almost anything you want
to know if they're sure you feel affection for them. This adds
to the trust that you won't reject them or use the information against them later. Express your affection openly,
strongly and frequently. The chapter on Romance gives
tips on how to do that.
      People are only going to be willing to show the "ugly"
side of them if they're sure that you already appreciate
their beautiful side. We all have a tendency to put our best
foot forward. The other foot only follows after we get the
message that someone has positive regard for us. If someone
shares information that you find disgusting or threatening in
some way, don't be afraid to share your feelings in a gentle
way. Hasten to add, however, that you still approve of them
despite any indiscretions or faults.

## REVEALING YOURSELF

      Another key to successful prying is self-disclosure.
The more you reveal about yourself, the more likely others
are to reciprocate. Self-disclosure is a must if you want to
avoid resentment from others when you pry. What kinds of
things should you reveal? Ideally, everything about you.
If you could open yourself totally to others, you probably
would be able to create the most intimate relationships on
earth. Realistically, however, we all have our secrets and
feel almost an overwhelming need to conceal at least some
of them. The wise course is to determine which secrets are
essential and which are expendable.

## EXERCISE
1.    Write down a list of secrets about yourself that you
      have never told anyone. Be sure that no one is around
      when you do this and rest assured that you can destroy
      the list at the completion of the exercise.

2.     Next to each secret, try to write down the name of at least one person with whom you would feel comfortable sharing the secret.

3.     If no one comes to mind, then write the name of the one person you least fear learning your secret. Imagine what their response would be if they knew. Would they stop liking you or become angry or violent? Would they blab the secret to someone else? If not, then why are you afraid of sharing this with them?

4.     Visualize telling the secret to a specific person. Would you feel more comfortable telling them over the phone, in person, or through the mail? When would you feel most comfortable revealing yourself? Rehearse the actual words you would say (out loud) until you feel comfortable with them.

5.     When you feel comfortable (or at least your discomfort is manageable), arrange to tell each secret to one or more persons. You may find it helpful to preface your revelation by telling the person that you have an important secret to share with them and that it's very hard for you to do so. Request a commitment that they will try not to laugh, become angry or be judgmental. Ask them to understand that the reason you're doing this is because you wish to be closer to them and that your secret is an obstacle to intimacy.

6.     You need not tell all of your secrets in one day or one week, but don't procrastinate. Your motivation may diminish with time so try to unburden yourself of your secrets as quickly as possible.

7.     After doing all this, make another list of secrets that you've shared with only one or a few people. Next to each secret write the names of one or more additional people you would feel comfortable knowing the secret.

Chuck is a 24 year old physicist. "My deepest secret was that I once had a male lover. I avoided telling anyone, even my oldest and dearest friend. That was the hardest, because I needed to tell someone and Burt was the logical person to start with. However, once he mentioned how sickened he was about the idea of men making love to men, so I figured it wasn't safe to tell him.

"One night the secret slipped out inadvertently. I was shocked to learn that Burt wasn't phased by it at all. The only thing he found surprising was that I had kept things secret for so long, since normally I'm very open with him."

This story expresses an important truth. Most of the time people won't find your secrets to be as demeaning as you do. People who care about you should be able to accept just about anything about you (unless you're an ax-murderer).

Some secrets, of course, may be wiser to conceal than reveal. Before telling a heavy secret, weigh the price you'll have to pay versus the gain in intimacy. For example, telling a lover that you have been unfaithful can result in more intimacy, but also in the termination of the relationship. Graphically describing your sexual experiences can produce more intimacy and even add sparks to your lovemaking, but it can also needlessly torture your present lover and cause strains in the relationship.

With strangers, you probably won't want to reveal any serious secrets. They might consider you to be a bit weird if you did. People you care for, on the other hand, make ideal listeners.

## SHARING SOMETHING NEGATIVE

One of the quickest ways to open the door to intimacy with someone you've just met is to share something negative. It's wise to ask for permission first. For example, "May I share something negative I feel about you?" Naturally you don't want to say something very offensive. Choose something that will have impact but won't nip a budding relationship. For example:

> I feel uncomfortable when you blow smoke in my direction.
> I feel like you aren't listening closely to me.
> I have the impression that you always come on this

way with women.

I feel you're being defensive with me.

I don't feel comfortable having your hand on my leg.

I would appreciate it if you ate this breath mint.

I think your shirt/blouse is too loud.

I don't think red is your best color.

I think you're making a mistake by hiding your beautiful hair in that awful hairdo.

Notice that all of these negative comments are "I" statements, which are less likely to offend someone. Sharing something negative soon after meeting a person can be risky. It's worth it, however, because it starts your relationship off on the right foot. Injecting intimacy into a relationship after dishonest patterns have developed is next to impossible. You may find it particularly difficult to share something negative with people who attract you strongly for fear of losing them. Actually those are the people with whom you most need to risk intimacy.

## FOUR LEVELS OF SELF-DISCLOSURE

There are four types of information you can reveal about yourself.

1.   Basic facts. This information is open to just about anybody. Normally you don't keep any of it secret. Included in this category are things like your name, where you work, the town where you live, the type of car you drive, your political affiliation, etc.

2.   Personal facts. You don't want to reveal this information to everyone. Being fired from a job, flunking school, or resisting the draft may be personal facts. If you're self-conscious about your age or weight, they too fall into this category.

3.   Past feelings. Your emotions are usually much more personal and intimate than facts. It is usually easiest to share feelings from the past, since you are now a different person to some extent and past feelings may now be somewhat obsolete. Nevertheless, sharing how you felt at various times in your life under varying

situations can be an important way of revealing yourself. Your feelings towards parents, siblings, other relatives, friends, bosses, subordinates, ex-spouses, and past lovers can still be very important (even if some of them are dead and no longer play an active role in your life).

4.  Present feelings. These are usually more personal than those from the past. They are, therefore, more difficult to share. It's much easier to say "I *used* to feel angry" than to say "I feel angry *now*." Also, it's easier to say, "I feel bitter towards my parents" than to say, "I feel bitter towards you." Remember, though, that the more difficult it is to reveal your feelings, the greater the increase of intimacy if you do so. While all four levels deepen intimacy, the crucial one is the last. Unfortunately, even after we feel close to people, we often limit ourselves to past feelings that have lost a great deal of their emotional charge. For example, "I was really mad at you last night when you were late" or "I was overwhelmed with love towards you when I saw you teach your daughter how to ride her bike." It's vital not to miss opportunities to share important feelings in the here and now, even if you feel a little vulnerable or embarrassed. Revealing your feelings later may be safer, but doesn't lead to much closeness.

## COMPLETE MESSAGES

A major obstacle to intimacy is only expressing part of a message. Ideally you share all of the following: 1) your view of the facts; 2) your opinions; 3) your feelings; 4) your needs and desires. For example, you tell your date, "It's getting late." This is only the tip of the iceberg. You're hoping that your date will get the message that you want to go home. If he/she is having a good time at the party, however, you may not get your needs met. You will probably wind up having to nag continuously for the next half hour, giving your date the silent treatment, or being hostile and cold on the ride home. Wouldn't it be wiser to share some of the following items?

| Facts: | It's midnight. I'm planning on getting up at 6 a.m. |
|---|---|
| Opinions: | This is a boring party. All of the interesting people have gone home. If I don't get home soon, I'll feel tired and cranky all day. |
| Feelings: | I feel bored and tired. I'm angry that you're enjoying yourself at a party I find dull. I'm afraid of how I'm going to feel tomorrow. |
| Needs: | I need to go home soon and go to bed. |

Another example is telling your date, "The food at that restaurant is kind of fattening." You're hoping your date will read between the lines and suggest another restaurant. If he/she doesn't get the message, you may end up eating at a place where you hate the food. You'll then feel resentful towards your date for not reading your mind and suggesting a better restaurant. It would be better to share some of the following information.

| Opinions: | The diet menu at that restaurant is tasteless. All of the delicious food has too many calories. |
|---|---|
| Feelings: | I hate that restaurant. |
| Desires: | I want to go to another restaurant. |

A third example of incomplete messages is telling your lover, "I resent your unwillingness to make love tonight." Your partner is likely to react in one of the following ways: 1) make love to you listlessly or resentfully; 2) refuse to make love and feel guilty. In either case, you're probably not going to get your needs met. Consider the option of sharing the following information.

| Facts: | That sexy movie we saw tonight really turned me on. |
|---|---|
| Opinions: | I'm going to have a hard time sleeping tonight unless we make love. |
| Needs: | I need to make love. |

The beauty of sharing this information is that your lover

knows what is going on inside of you. A lover who cares for you and isn't overly tired, drunk or apathetic probably will either attempt to satisfy you sexually or explain why that's not possible tonight.

## RULES FOR INTIMACY

1.  Don't expect people to know what you think, feel or need. This is called *Mindreading*, a power that none of us have. No one is responsible for reading your mind. Your obligation is to share what is going on inside of your head or suffer the consequences.

2.  Never assume you understand each other. There's an old joke that when you assume, you make an *ass* of *u* and *me*. Unless you're sure you have communicated clearly and effectively with one another, check things out. Don't be afraid of appearing foolish by repeating what you said if you suspect your friend may have missed your meaning. Better to be redundant than misunderstood. Likewise, don't be too embarrassed to ask your partner to repeat something.
    We're all imperfect speakers and listeners. Also, we often use the same words to convey different meanings. It's nor surprising, therefore, that miscommunication frequently occurs. Don't trust to chance. Your relationships are too precious for that.

3.  Express your feelings at appropriate times. For example, don't express your anger towards people after they've just been fired or discovered that a close relative died. Express your emotions at a time when the other person is going to be willing and able to hear and understand you.

4.  Express heavy feelings privately. Most people feel very embarrassed if you discuss personal things in front of others, particularly if you're criticizing them or expressing hostility. Wait until you're alone.

5.  Avoid asking questions when you're really making a statement.
    Don't ask:   Do you really want to make love tonight?

When you mean:   I don't want to make love tonight.
Don't ask:   Do you think this suit looks good on me?
When you mean: I'm afraid I'm getting fat.
Don't ask:   Do you love me?
When you mean:   I'm afraid that I'm losing you.
Don't ask:   Do you have to go out with the boys to-
             night?
When you mean:   I feel lonely tonight and would
             really appreciate your company.
Don't ask:   Do you think he's good looking?
When you mean:   I'm afraid you find him to be more
             attractive than I.

6.   Avoid double messages. For example, your lover asks,
     "Wouldn't it be great if we got married?" You reply,
     "I want to get married soon. By the way, did I tell you
     I may be laid off?" Here you're afraid to tell your
     lover that you don't want to get married so you men-
     tion the possibility of hard times ahead financially.
     You are conveying a contradictory, double message: I
     want to get married/I don't want to get married. If
     your lover only gets the message that you want to get
     married, you may end up being pressured into a
     marriage you don't want or having to explain later to
     a resentful partner why you're breaking your commit-
     ment. You'll both be happier in the long run if you
     communicate the truth: you don't want to be mar-
     ried.
         Another example is telling your lover, "I'm really
     turned on to you tonight. I sure wish I didn't have to
     get up early tomorrow." Here you don't have the
     courage to tell your lover that you don't want to make
     love, so you point out how inconvenient it would be
     for you. You are hoping this will get you off the hook.
     If your ploy doesn't work, you probably are going to
     be stuck with having sex and resenting it.

## DEALING WITH NEGATIVE FEELINGS
     "If you can't say something nice, then don't say
anything at all." Unfortunately, many of us were raised with
this proverb. Invariably we have negative feelings. There are
several things you can do with them.

1.    You can ignore them. This doesn't do any good. Feelings don't disappear—they just go underground. The frequent result is that you become irritated or depressed. You may feel dead or apathetic towards your friends, relatives and lovers. You also may suffer from anxiety, fear, or psychosomatic symptoms. These include ulcers, colds, aches, pains and illnesses. You may also eat, drink or take drugs excessively. In other words, the quality of your health and relationships both go down if you fail to acknowledge your true feelings.

2.    You can complain to others rather than the person who upsets you. This course has the advantage of making you feel better (you get negative feelings off your chest). Unfortunately, it doesn't change the offensive behavior. People will continue to act in ways that irritate you and you will continue to feel angry. An added disadvantage is that people may find out that you're complaining behind their backs and justifiably feel hostile towards you. Then they are even less willing to change their behavior.

3.    You can blow them away with your hostility (otherwise known as the "howitzer technique"). Dumping tremendous amounts of anger, criticism, and guilt seldom accomplishes anything constructive. If you succeed in tearing down their egos they will resent you all the more and resist change.

4.    You can express your negative thoughts and feelings in a healthy constructive way. The result is that you get the feelings off your chest *and* increase the possibility that the person will change. Most importantly, the level of intimacy goes up in your relationship.

One way to learn how to deal with negative emotions is to study what *not* to do. If your goal were to hurt people, provoke fights, or get them to close themselves emotionally to you, here are the secrets:

1.    Scream and yell. The louder the better.

2.   Use foul language.
3.   Make personal insults. The more names you call them and the lower the blows, the better. If possible, include their parents and friends.
4.   Make threatening gestures with your fists or objects. Kitchen knives are great props.
5.   Give a long list of criticisms. No negative quality or fault should be overlooked.
6.   Refer to other incidents that have upset you and add them to your immediate complaints. The longer you've known them the more ammunition you should be able to dredge up from the past.
7.   Hit 'em where it hurts. Concentrate on particularly painful areas of vulnerability. If they've been foolish enough to share their inadequacies or guilts, put special emphasis there.
8.   Sarcasm is extremely effective.
9.   Be brutally honest. There is a mean way and a nice way to say anything. Go out of your way to be vicious and then be sure to point out that "if the shoe fits, wear it."

Assuming you would prefer to be more loving and relate effectively with others, you may prefer to express negative emotions in as pleasant of a way as possible:

Instead of saying, "You're ugly," say "I'm not turned on to you."
Instead of saying, "You're fat," say "I like slimmer people."
Instead of saying, "You're all wrinkled," say "I like people who look younger."
Instead of saying, "You dress like a clown," say "Your colors don't match."
Instead of saying, "You're a basket case," say "I hope you're successful in overcoming some of your problems."
Instead of saying, "You're very lazy," say "I know you have trouble getting motivated to do things."

Notice that both ways of saying things are honest. The only difference is that one is more kind and loving than the other.

107

## HOW YOUR ACT PREVENTS INTIMACY

Being genuine is perhaps the greatest challenge in life. We have a tendency to devote much of our time "proving" our value to others. For example, Joan is a 22 year old skiing instructor. A good part of her conversation is usually devoted to boasting of all the men she has wrapped around her little finger. No one ever gets to know the real Joan—the one who has painful doubts about her physical attractiveness to men.

Martin is a 62 year old realtor. He constantly talks about how well his business is doing "while everyone else is going under." The real Martin is hidden—the part that fears his business will flop because he's a loser.

Rita is a 34 year old divorcee. She conceals her fear of frigidity by boasting of how passionate and uninhibited she is in bed. No one succeeds in penetrating her act and getting to know the real Rita.

John is a 29 year old electrician. His father is a college professor. He's the black sheep in the family because he's the only one who never went to college. In conversations, John always gets around to talking about the latest book he's reading, the fantastic documentary he saw on PBS, or the heavy message of the film he saw last night (naturally, a film with sub-titles). In reality, John hates to read and loves television situation comedies. No one ever finds this out.

Gail is a 53 year old supervisor. She pretends to be the most amiable person you'll ever meet. In her office, however, she's a tyrant who loves to run roughshod over the feelings of her subordinates, particularly men. She feels guilty about this and is careful to hide her dark side from friends with a sweetness and spice act. Consequently, no one ever makes intimate contact with her.

These are only a few examples of how we try to conceal our negative qualities in order to gain approval from others. What act is your favorite? The easiest way to find out is to ask yourself, what is the one impression I most fear making when I meet someone? Your act is probably built around pretending to be the opposite of one of the following qualities:

108

| 1. stupid | 8. mentally unbalanced |
|-----------|------------------------|
| 2. unattractive | 9. boring |
| 3. puritanical | 10. silly |
| 4. promiscuous | 11. too serious |
| 5. depressed | 12. selfish |
| 6. anxious | 13. cheap |
| 7. incompetent | 14. unfriendly |

Watch your next few conversations with new people. If you're honest with yourself, you'll likely notice that you often are a broken record, constantly repeating the same stories and facts in an effort to pull the wool over people's eyes and convince them that you are someone you're not. The antidote to this phoniness is simple:

1. Admit to yourself that you are not your act (e.g., you really aren't learned, sexy, brilliant, Marilyn Monroe, Florence Nightingale, Mother Teresa, Billy Graham, David Rockefeller, Tom Selleck or whomever or whatever you're pretending to be).

2. Tell people about your tendency to pretend to be the opposite of what you really are. Ask them to try to catch you each time you do this and point it out. Explain that you're tired of performing and want to make real contact with them.

Sometimes your act may not involve boasting or making a good impression. On the contrary, you may run yourself down and play one or more of the following roles: adultress, wanton woman, ignoramus, dummy, plain jane, Attila the Hun, liar, thief, pervert, neurotic. These negative roles are no more genuine than the positive ones. For example, Brenda is a 53 year old cafeteria worker. Her role is that of loser. She turns off almost all of the men she meets with her hour-long monologues about her physical, psychological, social and sexual problems. She does this to arouse sympathy and so no one will have high expectations of her.

1. She bores the people she meets.
2. She is as likely to receive their contempt as their sympathy.
3. She is uni-dimensional; all that people see is her loser

image.
4.     She rarely makes good contact with men.

Bob is a 48 year old window washer. His role is that of the incompetent bumbler who can't do anything for himself. He can't cook, shop, clean house, etc. Actually Bob is reasonably adept at all these things but hopes to attract a mother type who will take care of him. Rather than just express that need honestly, he wastes a great deal of his time playing the helpless role with women.

How do you run yourself down? What stories do you constantly repeat that show you in a bad light? As suggested earlier, tell your friends about your tendency to put on an act and ask them to reinforce your attempts to be more genuine with them.

## ARMOR

One of the most common acts is that of being so tough that nothing can harm you. If you play this role, the reason probably is that you are really very vulnerable to how people think and behave. Your act is designed to reassure you that you're not in danger. It also protects you from personal attacks, since "no one would dare attack somebody invulnerable like me."

The price you pay is that you must repress or hide all of your hurt feelings. These emotions don't disappear, however. They fester underneath the surface and trouble you until you deal with them honestly. In the meantime, no one is able to reach the vulnerable inner you. They remain at arm's length and you never achieve the intimacy you claim to want so badly.

## EXERCISE

Write down recent incidents when you concealed your hurt feelings from people. Tell each of them fully about the incident(s) and explain that the reason you acted as you did was to cover up your vulnerability.

Make an effort to share your fears, disappointments and frustrations with others. The more often you do this the easier it will become. Eventually you will get to the point where it's useless to hide your vulnerability because your friends and relatives already know about it. You will have

110

"graduated" when you are able to let people know when you feel hurt as it is actually happening.

## FISHING FOR COMPLIMENTS

Often we run ouselves down in order to encourage others to compliment us by disagreeing. For example, Mary successfully spends five hours making herself look gorgeous. She turns to her date and says, "I'm so jealous of all the beautiful women at this dance." The man naturally reassures her by remarking on how beautiful her face, hair and clothes are.

Another example: John mentions how embarrassing it is that his business "only" made $100,000 this year. His girlfriend dutifully replies that he is far more successful than most men.

The purpose of fishing for compliments is to avoid having to make them yourself and appear conceited. It is certainly true that you take a risk when you say positive things about yourself. Some people, particularly those with low self-esteem, may be offended if you appear to have a high opinion of yourself. That is *their* hangup. There is nothing wrong with feeling good about yourself and sharing this with others. If you only talk about your limitations, you are not giving people a complete picture of who you are. To be open means to share the positive as well as the negative. If you are afraid of being a braggard, ask yourself the following four questions:

1.   Do I lie about myself to improve my image?

2.   Do I exaggerate my good qualities?

3.   Do I conceal or deny my errors and negative qualities?

4.   Do I recite my good points ad nauseam?

Unless you habitually engage in these activities, don't worry about conceit. Share all of you, the good and the bad, and enjoy the resulting intimacy.

# LIES WE TELL OURSELVES

Intimacy with others requires intimacy with yourself. Otherwise, you will withhold important information about your thoughts and feelings because you are unaware of them. For example, Jill is a 20 year old lab technician. "My boyfriend, Sam, keeps asking me who I am. It's so irritating! He's always sharing his feelings with me and getting upset when I don't do the same. I tell him that I'm not holding back any secrets—that I'm telling him everything I know about myself."

Unfortunately, Jill is probably telling the truth. She really isn't holding anything back—from her boyfriend. She is concealing things from herself, however. Sam rightfully feels frustrated. The possibility of intimacy with Jill is seriously limited. Jill needs to become intimate with herself so she can share vital information with the men she meets.

Morgan is a 38 year old minister. "Jeanette, my last girlfriend, can be quite cruel. I was very intolerant of her at times when she was in a bitchy mood and unkind towards others. We used to get into big fights over this. She'd scream, 'Mind your own business!' Now that we're no longer together, I've had time to look at things calmly and rationally. I can see that the reason I was so intolerant of Jeanette was because I'm often cruel with people myself. I've been avoiding this truth for years."

There is an old cliche that we hate in others that which we hate most in ourselves. One way to become intimate with yourself is to observe what you find distasteful in others.

## EVADING REALITY

The worst lies are those we tell ourselves. While it's a myth that ostriches bury their heads in the sand when they are afraid, figuratively, this is what humans often do. When we're under stress or experience pain, we have a tendency to deny reality. Psychologists refer to defense mechanisms which enable us to avoid painful truths. Below are the eight most common ways we do this.

1. Repression. This is where you "blot out" painful thoughts and thrust them into your subconscious. For example, Jay is a 46 year old air force officer who refuses to acknowledge that he gets women drunk in order to engage in casual sex with them. Whenever women later accuse him of exploiting them, he erases the criticism from his consciousness in order to maintain his self-esteem.

2. Rationalization. This is where you avoid reality with "good reasons". For example, Mary is a college student who is ashamed of still being a virgin at age 23. She frequently dates but always refuses to have sex. Each time she gives herself a different excuse: I have to get up early tomorrow; I'm too tired; He'll think I'm cheap; He's just a Casanova. The truth that Mary is evading is that, unlike her roommate, she doesn't feel comfortable with the new morality.

3. Intellectualization. Here you avoid an unpleasant emotion by analyzing and experiencing it as a thought

113

rather than a feeling. For example, Phil is a 48 year old businessman who is bitterly upset over losing his girlfriend. He escapes the pain by analyzing how he feels and describing his pain in abstract terms, thereby losing contact with the emotion.

4.      Fantasy. Here you make believe that you are different than you really are. For example, David is an 18 year old bicycle repairman. He feels tongue-tied and shy around women and seldom has a date. Rather than confront his problem he pretends that he is suave and sophisticated and that the reason he doesn't succeed with women is because "chicks have no taste."

5.      Projection. This is where you accuse others of having thoughts, desires or feelings that actually are your own. For example, Sophia is a 28 year old woman who has never married. She calls her "friend" Francine a slut behind her back for occasionally engaging in casual sex. Actually, Sophia has one night stands, also. She avoids labeling herself as a "wanton woman" by accusing Francine.

6.      Blaming. Darlene is a 30 year old divorcee. She blames her children for her failure to remarry. If only they had been better behaved and nicer to her boyfriends, one of them would have married her. Actually, the true problem is her rotten disposition. After her disagreeable personality emerges in a relationship, her boyfriends dump her, as did her husband. Another example is Jan, a 35 year old divorced man. He has difficulty maintaining an erection because he drinks too much. He blames his girlfriend, Ellen, for being a "lousy lay". He thereby avoids facing the problem of his own impotence.

7.      Reaction formation. This is where you avoid acknowledging shameful parts of yourself by acting just the opposite. For example, Reggie is a 34 year old unemployed blue collar worker who has a "Don Juan complex". He has been repressing homosexual urges for many years and avoids facing the truth about his

sexual orientation by sleeping with numerous women each year, even if he finds them unattractive.

8.  Denial. Here you are evading reality by refusing to admit obvious facts. For example, Sue is a 39 year old commercial photographer. She refuses to acknowledge the fact that she is showing signs of aging. Her hair is graying, her breasts and other parts are sagging, and she has gained a few pounds. She still sees herself as a beautiful young woman in her twenties rather than as a still attractive person who is approaching middle age.

These are only some of the ways we avoid reality. It would be nice if lying to yourself worked—if you could actually avoid pain through self-deception. Unfortunately, no matter how hard you try, you can never fully submerge the truth. Somewhere deep in your subconscious you retain the hidden facts. Inevitably the truth slips out and you must constantly re-deceive yourself in order to keep it down. Shakespeare once wrote that a "coward dies a thousand deaths—a brave man but once." Nowhere is this more true than with lying to yourself. A woman who knows she is plain-looking may attempt to deceive herself into believing that she is beautiful. She may resort to sleeping with countless men in an effort to prove her sexual attractiveness. How much happier she would be if she faced the reality of her lack of beauty, however painful it might temporaily be. Instead, she spends the rest of her life vainly attempting to fool herself.

Another problem that arises when you deny reality is that it prevents you from making important changes. So long as you refuse to face a problem, it will persist and you will have to experience the pain that accompanies it. For example, a woman can deny that her husband no longer loves her but this doesn't change the fact that she is unloved. So long as she denies reality, she is unable to change her marriage and get her emotional needs met.

How can you stop lying to yourself and learn to face reality? First, you must become aware of the fact that reality cannot be denied and that the price of self-deception is misery. The next step is to catch yourself in the act of lying.

This is not easy. After spending many years avoiding reality, you probably are quite adept at it. Only by patient self-examination can you uncover your self-deception. The next time you feel uncomfortable, psychologically ask yourself, "What am I hiding from myself?" This is not to say that psychological pain is necessarily a sign of self-deception, but only that it is a time when you are most tempted to avoid reality.

**EXERCISE**

1. List all of the criticisms, complaints, and insults you can remember receiving that have bothered you. Each of us has a long list of gripes we have heard from others that make us uncomfortable. The only reason they bother us is because to some extent we believe they are true. A truly ridiculous criticism like, "You're too fat" will slide right off a skinny person. "You're a lousy tennis player" wouldn't have much of an effect on Jimmy Connors.

   After you have listed all of the insults that make you feel touchy, you are in a beautiful position to uncover self-deception. If you are a normal person, for years you have been repressing, rationalizing, intellectualizing, denying, or otherwise avoiding these truths about yourself. How liberating it would be to say, "yes, it's true that I have a bad temper" or "yes, I do sometimes act recklessly," rather than spend a lifetime lying to yourself.

2. For each negative comment about yourself on your list, ask yourself, "Am I trying to avoid reality through:

   * Repression (blotting out reality and thrusting painful thoughts into my subconscious)?
   * Rationalization (convincing myself that something I know to be false is actually true)?
   * Intellectualization (killing my emotions by analyzing and experiencing them as thoughts rather than feelings)?
   * Fantasy (making believe I'm different than who I really am)?
   * Projection (accusing others of having thoughts, de-

sires, or feelings that actually are my own)?
- Blame (blaming others for my problems)?
- Reaction formation (avoiding knowledge of shameful things about myself by acting just the opposite)?
- Denial (refusing to admit the facts)?

Sensitivity to criticism doesn't necessarily mean that the criticism is valid. Quite often if you study a troublesome insult, you discover that it isn't correct. If, after honest evaluation, you conclude that you aren't "too selfish" or "inconsiderate" or "incompetent" or "dumb", you will be less sensitive the next time you are insulted.

Some of the lies that singles tell themselves are particularly detrimental to developing loving relationships with the opposite sex. Single men frequently deceive themselves with the following statements.

1.  I'm here to meet women. If you tell yourself this lie, you claim you want to meet women, yet at social events all you do is eat, drink, talk to men or talk to women you find unattractive (and, therefore, safe). If you truly are there to meet women, you will do exactly that. Instead, you lie to yourself and thereby avoid the need to overcome your fear of meeting women.

2.  Women only want one thing. Supposedly the one thing that all women want is money. If you are afraid of initiating contact with women, you may use this lie as an excuse for shyness. It is true that many women consider money to be a major priority when meeting men but it's also true that many of them are not terribly concerned about a man's financial status. If you are a man of modest means, your job is to locate this second type of woman and initiate contact, rather than lie to yourself.

3.  Women are all bitches. Here you are attempting to justify your ineffectiveness in relationships with women. You don't have to own up to your own shortcomings if women are naturally sickening. It is true that many women (like men) have rotten dispositions.

117

It is also true, however, that there are more who are sweet and lovable. Your task is to separate the wheat from the chaff. Lying to yourself only impedes this process.

Women are equally adept at lying to themselves. Some of their favorite lies follow.

1. I'm here to meet men. If you tell yourself this lie, you claim you want to meet someone nice and then do everything in your power to prevent this from happening. You purposely seat yourself away from all the action (where the men are). You surround yourself with women. You refuse to make eye contact with any of the men across the room who may gaze or smile at you. And, of course, you never, never initiate contact with men. Then you can't understand why you never meet anyone!

2. All men are bastards. This is no more true than the male counterpart: all women are bitches. It does provide an excuse, however, for staying home or avoiding contact with me. It is important to face the reality that a man is *not* a "bastard" because:

   - he falls out of love with you
   - he tires of you
   - he gets angry
   - he is critical of your faults
   - he leaves you for someone else more attractive
   - he is attracted to other women
   - he doesn't meet your needs
   - he doesn't live up to your expectations.

   Every man (just as every woman) has the right to be himself and work to meet his own needs. His obligations to you are secondary.

3. I will reform him. It's amazing how many women marry alcoholics, wife-beaters or other losers expecting to reform them, as if a wedding ring bestows magical powers. "All he needs is a good woman" is

the battlecry. In reality, husbands have the same short-comings as they did before they walked down the aisle. If anything, his irritating qualities are likely to become more intolerable as each year goes by and your patience wears thinner.

Most men (as well as women) are either unable or unwilling to change their negative qualities. Your encouragement and assistance may help him make changes, but the odds are against significant reform. One thing is sure: your nagging and complaining will only make matters worse. You will join the millions of miserable, antagonistic couples who are constantly fighting the losing battle of remaking people.

4. White charger. With this lie, you claim that all the men you meet are losers, but somewhere out there is the man who is handsome, strong, wealthy, witty, faithful, and flawless. Those men do not exist. If you expect the man on the white charger to come along, you are in for a long, lonely wait.

5. Men only want one thing. Men *don't* only want sex. "Playboys" are like everyone else: they want love, intimacy, joy and security. They also want sex, but that isn't unusual for human beings. Casual sex is an important priority to many men but only a small percentage feel satisfied with sex alone. Claiming that men only want one thing can provide you with the excuse to be cold, withdrawn and defensive with them. Like the other lies in this chapter, it can insure that you never meet someone special.

## SELF-ESTEEM

Earlier exercises in this chapter will help you become more intimate with yourself, but they don't strike at the root cause of self-deception: a lack of self-esteem. Society teaches us to strive to be better than we are. Success, achievement, ambition, self-actualization and reaching for your potential are all glorified by our culture. Being satisfied with who you are is not so highly regarded. The next exercise will enable you to determine how dissatisfied you are with yourself.

## EXERCISE

Mark a check next to each statement with which you agree:

___ I should be a better person.
___ I should be more ethical.
___ I should be more talented.
___ I should be more loving.
___ I should be more successful.
___ I should be harder working.
___ I should be more dependable.
___ I should be more interesting.
___ I should be better educated.
___ I should make more money.
___ I should be a better lover.
___ I should be married.
___ I should be more intelligent.
___ I should be a better son/daughter.
___ I should be a better mother/father.
___ I should have a better personality.
___ I should be more honest.
___ I should be more loyal.
___ I should be more generous.
___ I should be more attractive.
___ I should be better coordinated.
___ I should lose weight.
___ I should exercise more.
___ I should follow the advice in this book.

Where do all your "shoulds" come from? Originally you got them from your parents:

> I should clean my plate.
> I should be a good boy/girl.
> I should do my homework.
> I should get good grades.

Later you picked up obligations from your relatives, friends, teachers, priests/ministers/rabbis, gurus, bosses, fellow employees, lovers, spouses, children, strangers, and, of course, society at large.

One tragedy is that frequently the shoulds are contradictory: mom wants you to be a doctor, dad wants you to be a football player or ballerina; one lover wants you to be more aggressive, the other more passive; one friend accuses you of being too selfish, the other criticizes your over-generosity. In other words, trying to live up to the expect-tations of others is a no-win situation.

Some of the shoulds you learn are impossible:

I should be perfect.
I should always tell the truth.
I should never be selfish.
I should always win.

Sometimes people manipulate you with shoulds so that you serve their interests rather than your own:

You should visit your mother every day.
You should earn more money (so I can have a new car).
You should get a college degree (so I can brag to my friends about you).

You can spend the rest of your life vainly trying to live up to all the expectations and goals others have established for you (or you have set for yourself). A wiser course is to dump all the shoulds and accept yourself as you are.

I learned this lesson one weekend several years ago at Esalen, the world-famous growth center in California. I greatly admired a middle-aged gentleman in the group who had a very positive air about him. At the end of the weekend, I complimented him on his self-esteem and was shocked by his answer. "I don't think highly of myself. I am well aware of my many shortcomings and don't let them bother me. I am happy being exactly who I am."

This self-acceptance, not achievement or change, is the key to self-esteem. Give up trying to be what you are *not* and just accept who you *are*. There's nothing wrong with trying to change things for the better—as long as you don't feel obligated to do so. There's nothing wrong with striving to become a better person—as long as this is not a condition for self-esteem. Self-improvement is good—if it is built on a core of self-acceptance.

As a former hard-driving, perfectionistic, self-critical

121

individual I can testify to the debilitating effect these qualities can have on self-esteem. Learn to accept yourself unconditionally: whether you are sinner or saint, scholar or ignoramus, good-looking or homely. Accept yourself and you have achieved the highest good you can attain.

**EXERCISE**

Make a list of all of your negative qualities. Be very specific. If necessary, look at the list of shoulds earlier in this chapter. If you are unable to come up with dozens of shortcomings, call up your parents, relatives, friends, etc. They will be able to double or triple the size of your list. When you have a list that is sufficiently large (or you run out of ink), read each quality slowly and ask yourself, "Can I live with myself if I am like this for the rest of my life?" If you can answer yes to each item on your list, you have the world by the tail. If not, write down the following preface for each negative quality on your list: "I have the right to be _____." For example, "I have the right to be unreliable."

Self-esteem does more than enable you to become intimate with yourself and, therefore, others. It is crucial to meeting someone special for two reasons. First, if you value yourself, others are more likely to find you attractive. Bad-mouthing yourself is infectious—people will believe you if you claim to be inferior. Secondly, self-esteem gives you the confidence to go after people you find attractive. It makes you feel you deserve to be in a relationship with an attractive person, also. Even if you are rejected, your self-esteem will enable you to shrug off a momentary setback and continue to initiate contact with attractive people.

Years ago, I did graduate work on self-esteem and developed exercises for use with children in the classroom. The exercises involved discovering your good points, listing them on paper and sharing them with others. I have resisted the temptation to share these exercises with you because I believe they have a self-defeating premise: that you have to be "good" in order to have self-esteem. What's so bad about being bad? In other words, why not just be yourself and not worry about it?

# GAMES SINGLES PLAY

Since most of us place a great premium on openness, honesty, and intimacy, why is there so much dishonesty between men and women? According to behaviorist theory, we all tend to do things for which we are rewarded and tend not to do that for which we are punished. If this is true then the reason for so much dishonesty is that we are punished when we tell the truth and rewarded when we lie. We can all think of examples: the man who tells a woman the truth, that he only wants a casual sexual relationship, is likely to go home alone; the man who lies and tells her he loves her is likely to win a bed partner. The flat-chested woman may go unnoticed at a party; the woman wearing "falsies" has a much greater chance of attracting attention.

If you find yourself writing off the opposite sex because they're all playing too many games, you need to learn to be more tolerant of dishonesty. A first step is to admit that we all are liars—some of the time. It's amazing how many people say that they never lie. Who do they think they're fooling? Probably only themselves. They can't face the fact that they are human beings and, therefore, lie—just like everyone else. People who freely admit to being fat, lousy listeners, or unreliable, will not admit that they are sometimes dishonest.

Most people lie when they are frightened or when it enables them to achieve an important objective, such as money, sex, or love. To expect people to do otherwise is to "dream the impossible dream." This makes for good theater

123

but doesn't often happen in relationships. Completing the next exercise will give you a good picture of how honest you are.

**EXERCISE**

1. I tell the complete truth on my income tax forms (a) always ___ (b) most of the time ___ (c) seldom ___.
2. When people ask my opinion about their haircuts or clothing, I tell the truth (a) almost always ___ (b) most of the time ___ (c) seldom ___
3. When people ask if I enjoyed the dinner, movie, concert, etc. they arranged for us to experience, I answer truthfully (a) almost always ___ (b) most of the time ___ (c) seldom ___
4. When people ask about my feelings towards them, I am honest (a) almost always ___ (b) most of the time ___ (c) seldom ___
5. I share my anger with those around me (a) almost always ___ (b) most of the time ___ (c) seldom ___.
6. I share my depression with those around me (a) almost always ___ (b) most of the time ___ (c) seldom ___.
7. I share my shame or embarrassment with those around me (a) almost always ___ (b) most of the time ___ (c) seldom ___
8. I share my fears with those around me (a) almost always ___ (b) most of the time ___ (c) seldom ___

What is your reaction to the information you just learned about yourself? Is it embarrassing? If you're having a difficult time accepting your dishonesty, perhaps it will help to adopt the following policy: Everyone has the right to lie about themselves. In other words, you are not obligated to share your true feelings or reveal information about yourself. Lying about other things may be morally reprehensible, but lying about yourself is your inalienable right.

Having the right to lie doesn't mean that it's always to your advantage to be dishonest. As a general rule, the more you are authentic and share your thoughts and feelings, the more comfortable you are likely to feel, the healthier you are likely to be and the more intimacy you will develop in your relationships. When you lie, you tend to become uptight, feel frustrated and lower your level of intimacy. Your lies keep you apart from others, never feeling known and understood, never feeling total trust. The degree of honesty in a relationship is quite often a gauge of its quality.

Honesty is *not* always the best policy, however. It's puzzling that so many unfaithful men and women tell their spouses or lovers about their infidelity. Unless the couple has an agreement that each can step out on the other (in which case, they're not really being unfaithful), such a policy is frequently suicidal for the relationship. For better or worse, most of us can't handle infidelity. The Simenauer & Carroll survey discovered that three-quarters of singles considered infidelity to be grounds for ending a relationship.

If you desire more honesty in your relationships, there are two secrets: 1) be as honest as possible yourself; 2) reward others when they are honest with you. Each time you punish people who tell you the truth (for example, by being angry), you increase the chances that they will lie to you the next time. The following exercise will enable you to discover how accepting you are of the truth.

**EXERCISE**

Even if people speak to me in a respectful manner and are not trying to hurt me, I still feel angry when they tell me:

1. They are upset or angry with me. a) almost always ____ b) often ____ c) seldom ____
2. They don't like what I'm wearing. a) almost always ____ b) often ____ c) seldom ____
3. They don't like my new haircut, hairstyle, or hair coloring. a) almost always ____ b) often ____ c) seldom ____
4. They think I am overweight, below average in physical appearance, or unattractive in some way. a) almost always ____ b) often ____ c) seldom ____
5. They criticize something I've done. a) almost always ____ b) often ____ c) seldom ____
6. They mention some ability or talent I lack. a) almost always ____ b) often ____ c) seldom ____

If you marked almost always or often to several of these items, people are likely to tell you want you want to hear, rather than the truth. They either lie or withhold truths that they feel you can't handle.

The ironic thing about requiring honesty is that even if you did meet someone totally honest, you probably couldn't handle it. You live in a society where you are usually cushioned from the negative thoughts and feelings people have towards you. You might not enjoy overdosing on the truth.

What are some of the dishonest games singles play? Some of the more common ones follow.

## CATCH YOU NEXT TIME

This is a game both sexes love to play. Suppose a man and woman meet by chance and establish immediate rapport. After talking, eating or dancing together for an hour or two, the moment of truth arrives when they will separate. The man and woman face each other sheepishly, each agonizing on whether or not to risk rejection by suggesting a future meeting. One of them bravely makes a feeble pass: "It sure was nice meeting you." The other person drops the ball by responding, "Yeah, catch you next time."

If in the last 20 or more years you never saw this person before, what are the odds that you'll bump into each other again? A golden opportunity passes by because neither of you is willing to be honest. Having the courage to initiate contact and good conversation skills are not enough. All is wasted unless you're willing to take a chance and ask to see the person again. If you wish, you may exchange phone numbers but this is a risky process. Many singles fail to contact each other after such a transfer. The best thing to do is set a definite time and place to meet each other again (in other words, a date). If people are unwilling to make a definite commitment to see you, chances are the game being played is POSTPONEMENT. They really aren't interested in you romantically and don't have the guts to tell you, so they buy you off with a telephone number. The expectation is that you'll never call. If you do call, you will hear numerous excuses for not going out with you. Eventually you get the message but not until after a great deal of frustration and a sense of rejection.

I have a policy that irritates many women. I don't accept the phone numbers of women I meet who are unwilling to make a definite commitment to get together again. I don't enjoy being rejected over the telephone so I only call women I believe are genuinely interested in me. If they are unwilling to set a date, I assume that the odds are they find me unattractive. If they insist that they really do want to get together with me again, I hand them my card and suggest that they call me. They never do, which proves my point.

## I'M PERFECT

If you play this game, you are convinced that if anyone really knew you, the result would be rejection. It's true that revealing your true self is risky—you often will be rejected. Hiding your faults and appearing closed and phony are also likely to result in being turned down, however. The wise course is to gradually reveal negative parts of yourself along with putting your best foot forward.

## GAMES MEN PLAY WITH WOMEN

1. *Wedding Ring.* As pointed out earlier, married men frequently take off their wedding rings in order to masquerade as single men. Any woman who is victimized by a married man usually has only herself to blame. Before going out with a guy, check him out. You don't have to hire Jim Rockford to determine if he's single. Just ask for his phone number so you can call him before your first date. If a woman answers, don't hang up and assume the worse. Find out if she's his daughter, mother or platonic roommate.

2. *Out of towner.* Traveling salesmen, vacationers, or men at business conventions sometimes pretend to be locals. Follow the same advice as that for *Wedding Ring.* Ask for the man's phone number and call him before your first date. If a hotel or motel switchboard operator answers, you know that the guy is from out of town and looking for a "quick score".

3. *Doctor/Lawyer.* Every man knows that mothers tell their daughters to marry a doctor or lawyer. The temptation to be an imposter is, therefore, great. Women can protect themselves by asking where a man works and calling to verify. You don't have to

identify yourself when you call the man's office. Get the verification you need and say goodbye.

4.  *Seduction.* Men have perfected this game over thousands of years. The most popular version is "I Thought You Loved (Liked) Me." Here a woman is asked to prove her affection by going to bed with a man. There is no automatic connection between liking someone and having sex, but millions of women have fallen for this line over the years. A woman has every right to label this as emotional blackmail and refuse to do anything she finds uncomfortable.

## GAMES WOMEN PLAY WITH MEN

1.  *Women's Lib.* Any women who claim to be liberated show their true colors when the check arrives. Being liberated, as Phyllis Schlafly is quick to point out, has its liabilities. It would be wise for men to realize that we still live in a sexist society and that old traditions die slowly. A woman's actions speak more loudly than her words.

2.  *I Don't Go To Bed On The First Date.* There are two common variations to this game. The first is where the woman finds a man unattractive or simply isn't in the mood for sex. Rather than say so, she claims that she has a policy of not engaging in casual sex. Men usually have no way of judging her sincerity (since many women do genuinely follow this policy). Most of them really don't care. The bottom line is that they aren't going to get their sexual needs met that night, which is what concerns them.

    The second variation is where women use the same line but break down and engage in sex anyway. Tom, a 30 year old television repairman, provides this insight: "I always have to bite my tongue to keep from laughing when I wake up in bed with a woman and she proceeds to tell me that she doesn't ever do this with other guys. I have no delusions about being God's gift to women. I figure that if a chick sleeps with me the first time we meet, she probably does the same with other guys."

3.  *Hard to Get*. The purpose of this game is to prove how desirable you are by having men chase you. Besides being ego-gratifying, this game supposedly has the advantage of meeting a man's need for the thrill of conquest. Women who play this game argue that men don't value women who come too easily. This is often true, but consider the price you pay by playing hard to get: all the men you lose who find you attractive but aren't willing to pursue you.

4.  *Stand-up*. A man shows up at a woman's door ready for an enjoyable evening, only to find that she isn't there. I was once victimized by this game and vowed never again. A man is silly if he doesn't call to confirm a first date with a woman.

You probably feel resentful when singles play these games with you. The next chapter tells you how to deal with these and other resentments.

# RESENTMENTS

Resentments can sabotage your relationships. If you think you're doing all the right things but still aren't developing the loving relationship you want, the culprit may be your resentments. The first half of this chapter deals with female resentments. It's important for men to read this half even though it is directed towards women. Their anger (repressed or overt) is poisoning their relationships with men like you. Read the resentments as objectively as you can. "If the shoe fits, wear it." If you want to have successful, happy relationships with women, it may be to your advantage as well as theirs to own up to your shortcomings and attempt to change.

**EXERCISE (for women only)**
1.     List all the things you can't stand about men. Be specific.

2.     Next to each resentment, write down the names of ex-husbands or ex-boyfriends who had these negative qualities.

3.     Look at each resentment from a male perspective and see if you can understand why some men act this way.

4.     Again, looking at your list, determine your own role in causing or encouraging men to act in these ways. Go down your list and circle the resentments that you

honestly expressed to ex-lovers. Take responsibility for the uncircled resentments. Men are not mind readers. Possibly if you had complained to them (without nagging or hostility), they would have been willing to change. Unless you shared your negative feelings with them, you never gave them a chance.

Each of the women quoted below has a different resentment. Probably some of them are on your list. As you read them, try to realize that resentments don't add anything to your life. They just make it harder for you to connect with a loving man.

SHARI: "The thing I hate most about men is that they're only after sex. I like sex but there are a lot of other important things, like romance, intimacy, affection, good conversation. I'm not interested in just being another notch on a guy's belt. I wish guys would drop their high school scoring games and relate to women as people first and sex objects second."

JULIE: "Why is it that every guy I meet wants to jump right into bed. I like to get to know a guy first. There's nothing worse than waking up in the morning next to some strange man and not even remember his name."

It's true that men tend to glorify casual sex. They have been conditioned to prove their manhood by "scoring" with different women. Some anthropologists suggest that modern men satisfy their prehistoric hunter's instinct by chasing and capturing women.

Whatever the reason, most men appear to be obsessed with casual sex. Russell Clark, a Florida State professor, conducted experiments where his male and female psychology students approached members of the opposite sex and asked them, "Would you like to go to bed with me?" Not a single woman said yes, while 75% of the men agreed to go to bed with a complete stranger. Most of the men who rejected the offer politely explained that they were married or in a serious relationship.

It is normal to resent the male predilection for casual sex. It is also futile. Men aren't going to change no matter how resentful you feel. As long as they are conditioned to desire casual sex, that's the way they're going to be. Rather than get upset, why not just accept the harsh reality, like death and taxes? Just make sure that you don't allow men to pressure you into something you won't enjoy.

ELAINE: "Guys are really gross. I'm not interested in hearing their locker room talk. Somebody should clue them in on how to act around a lady. What really burns me up is the strangers who ask me to dance and then take liberties with me."

Men have been conditioned to believe that foul language is "manly" so naturally they have a tendency to verbally show off their masculinity. If a man's language offends you, tell him. The same holds true for gross actions. If he persists, move away.

RHONDA: "I can't stand all the seduction games men play. You wouldn't believe how many guys say they love me or tell me how special I am after a 15 minute conversation. Five minutes later I hear them use the same line on the next woman."

Many men try insincerity in the hopes of seducing women. They do it because it works—many women are easy marks for a man who knows how to flatter and tell them what they want to hear. The secret to dealing with make-out artists is to spot them and get rid of them as soon as possible so you can meet the many sincere men who want to get to know you.

JUNE: "Isn't there anybody out there who still believes in romance? What ever happened to giving a girl flowers or candlelight dinners or bringing a nice bottle of wine?"

Let your boyfriends know that you appreciate a touch of romance. Don't expect them to be mindreaders.

OPHELIA: "I can't stand guys who watch or talk sports 24 hours a day. Have you ever watched a baseball game that's a no-hitter? It's got to be the most boring way on earth to spend three hours! Football and hockey have more action— but they're so violent. I can't understand how anyone can be fascinated with the sight of some man beating another guy's brains out. While we're on the subject, everybody knows that men start all the wars. This world would be a lot better off if women were in control."

Women frequently are mystified by men's glorification of sports, violence and warfare. Just remember that if you had been raised as a man, you'd probably feel the same way. Men can't understand how women can "waste" hours shopping for new clothes, their fascination with jewelry, and a host of other things.

JAMIE: "Men are too superficial. There's more to me than my physical appearance and I resent guys who treat me as a sex object."

This indictment of men is well-taken, but think how you would feel if men *didn't* find you to be attractive. Count your blessings.

BETSY: "Guys are too pushy. Why can't they take no for an answer?"

Many men were raised to believe that a woman automatically said no to save her "honor," but really wanted sex as much as they did. They learned to ignore the obligatory no until it turned into a yes. Obviously they wouldn't persist in being pushy unless it works sometimes. Alex is a 47 year old used car salesman. "I love it when my dates tell me early in the evening that there's no way they're going to bed with me. I know automatically that I'm going to score with them that night. It never fails!"

With the exception of rapists, men do take no for an answer—but you sometimes have to be very firm. Try to avoid three things that encourage men to be overly-aggressive:

1.  Sudden coldness. If you kiss, embrace, and touch a man intimately all night, you're crazy if you think you can suddenly turn him off. Don't start something you don't want to finish.

2.  Saying no when your body means yes. A man tends to believe what you do more than what you say. You negate the power of your words if you snuggle up to a man at the same time you are supposedly trying to get rid of him.

133

3.    Sexual innuendos. Don't make subtle suggestions and no-so-subtle jokes about sex and then wonder why men don't believe you when you say you don't want to make love.

LUCY: "Men are lousy lovers. All they want to do is rush things. Whatever happened to cuddling and foreplay?"

It is sad but true that many men don't enjoy hugging, kissing, and touching. Their sexuality is limited to intercourse. If you find yourself with someone like this, try to educate him concerning the joys of foreplay. Tell him, "Try it, you might like it." If that doesn't work, you have to either lump it or dump him. There are millions of men in this country who excel in foreplay.

INGRID: "I'm sick and tired of slam, bam, thank you, ma'am. Men shouldn't be so selfish. I have needs too, you know. Those guys should learn how to exercise a little self-control and wait until I'm satisfied."

This is the Myth of the Quick Shooter. Supposedly there's something wrong with a man if he ejaculates quickly during sexual intercourse: he is sick, abnormal, immature, selfish or incompetent. The fact of the matter is that the average man in the United States ejaculates from 30 seconds to 2½ minutes after the beginning of intercourse. In other words, it is biologically *normal* for a man to achieve orgasm far more quickly than a woman. If you resent some men for being quick-shooters, you are expecting them to act abnormally.

As mentioned before, it is important for men to learn to enjoy foreplay so women are "warmed up" for intercourse. In addition, sex therapists such as Masters and Johnson are quite adept at teaching couples to change their lovemaking patterns so they are more fulfilling for both partners. If sexual problems arise, you don't have to live with them. Seek professional help.

SANDY: "I can't stand the old double standards. Why is it okay for my boyfriend to sleep around but wrong for me to do the same?"

Why indeed? Rather than feel resentful, take personal responsibility for this inequity. The only men who successfully maintain a double standard are those with women weak enough to tolerate it. There is nothing to prevent you from standing up for equal rights and upholding the same standards of loyalty (or disloyalty) that your lover does.

VIRGINIA: "Men are such babies. I already have two kids and resent being forced into the role of mother to my lovers."

Nobody forces you into playing a maternal role. If you do so, it is by choice.

COLLEEN: "The one thing I can't take in a man is insensitivity. I like a man who is into his feelings and can express love, affection and sorrow. How come I keep running into emotional cripples who never share their feelings with me?"

This complaint is well-taken. It's important to realize, however, that men in America are conditioned to imitate the Gary Cooper type and be strong, composed and silent. Men who cry are called sissies. Rather than resent men for this, feel some compassion. Sidney Jourard, in his book *The Transparent Self*, argues that the main reason men die so much earlier than women is because they bottle up their feelings.

Feel lucky if you find it easy to express your feelings. There are millions of men who are valiantly struggling to break out of their emotional strait jackets. Encourage them. If you can't handle the frustration of relating to men who are insensitive and emotionally cold, rensentment is not the answer. Limit yourself to dating the minority of men who are emotionally liberated.

LAURA: "What gets me mad is attractive men I meet who ask for my phone number and don't call. It's awfully frustrating to be waiting all week for a call that never comes. If he wasn't planning on calling then why did he copy down my number in the first place?"

There are several possible explanations:

1. He lost your phone number.
2. He didn't remember you after he sobered up.
3. He collects phone number, like trophies, to prove his manhood.
4. He is afraid of your rejecting him when he calls.

5.    You are seldom if ever home and he keeps missing you.

You can easily get rid of your resentments in this area by asking for a man's number every time you give him yours and calling him unless he reaches you first. Purchasing a telephone answering machine can also be a big help if you are often out of the house. A man will call only so many times before giving up and calling some other lucky woman.

MAY:    "The guys I hate most are the ones that stand you up. It's happened to me a couple of times and it's infuriating."
Why do men stand women up? The three most likely reasons are:

1.    He forgot.
2.    He changed his mind and didn't have your phone number to cancel.
3.    He changed his mind and didn't have the courage to tell you.

You can easily protect yourself from these possibilities by exchanging phone numbers and calling him to confirm the date the night before (unless he's already called you first).

**EXERCISE**
A good way to get over your resentments is to play a game called VICTIM.

1.    Ask a close friend or relative to help you play.

2.    Choose a resentment where you feel victimized by a man: "He done me wrong."

3.    Tell your friend to encourage you to relate all the rotten things your victimizer did to you. Don't be afraid of character assassination. Be totally one-sided. Your friend's job is to cheer you on as you let your victimizer have it with both barrels.

4.    After you feel finished, switch sides. This time ex-

136

plain to your friend how *you* are totally responsible for the problem. Explain how you created the situation and added "fuel to the fire". Your friend's role is to encourage you to blame yourself for the sorry predicament.

This is a very powerful exercise. You will realize that "it takes two to tango" and that to a large extent you are responsible for your problems with men. Playing VICTIM will enable you to let go of some of your resentment so you free yourself of excess baggage as you search for Mr. Right.

## MALE RESENTMENTS
Men have equally strong resentments towards women. If you are a woman, it is important to read this section and discover why men often resent you. If you are honest with yourself, you'll admit that you engage in some of the negative behaviors described below. It is in your best interest to attempt to change.

## EXERCISE (for men only)
1.  List all the things you can't stand about women. Be very specific.

2.  Next to each resentment, write down the names of ex-wives or ex-girlfriends who had these negative qualities.

3.  Look at each resentment from a female perspective and see if you can understand why some women act this way.

4.  Again, looking at your list, determine your own role in causing or encouraging women to act in these ways. Go down your list and circle the resentments you honestly expressed to ex-lovers. Take responsibility for the uncircled ones. Women are not mind readers. Possibly if you had complained to them (without nagging or hostility), they would have been willing to change. Unless you shared your negative feelings with them, you never gave them a chance.

Now read about the resentments explained below. Probably some of them are on your own list. The most important thing to realize is that resentments don't add anything to your life; they just make it harder for you to connect with a loving woman.

GORDON: "Why are women always on the defensive? It seems like whenever I walk up to one she acts like I'm a rapist. Why can't women relax and be friendly? You'd think they would welcome a sincere single man who approaches them."

It is true that many women are on the defensive. They have good reason to be. Men are bigger, stronger and more violent than women. If you have difficulty understanding why women are intimidated by men, do the following exercise.

**EXERCISE**

This is a science fiction exercise. Imagine you are part of an all-male crew sent to a distant galaxy. You arrive on a planet where the average women is five inches taller than you, outweighs you by 40 pounds, and has biceps twice your size. While you are on the planet, two of your fellow crew members are raped. One of them dies from strangulation. Visualize yourself in a dark alley with one of these Amazons. How do you feel?

The next time you feel resentful towards an overly-defensive or negative woman, imagine how many jerks have walked up to her and been crude, phony or obnoxious. Perhaps you will then better understand why women are not always friendly to strangers. Don't take it personally. You may be guilty of poor timing (approaching her two minutes after a jerk). Go on to the next attractive woman.

The best way to get women to relax and be friendly is to smile warmly. Don't touch her initially; she may feel threatened. Move slowly and let her get used to you gradually. Once she discovers you don't have horns, the possibility arises for a good relationship.

DARRYL: "Women are hung up about sex. Most of them think it's dirty. They should learn to enjoy sex just for fun

138

sometimes instead of always worrying about whether or not they know me well enough. Sex isn't something sinful that has to be sanctified by love or marriage."

Women definitely tend to have a very different attitude than men towards casual sex. Despite today's free love rhetoric, most women still believe that sex should be "meaningful". Sex for the sake of sex isn't enough. While most women don't require a wedding ring, they prefer sex in the context of a committed relationship or at least a casual friendship. For example, Cecilia is a 24 year old chemist. "I've had a few one night stands in my life. I can't say I didn't enjoy myself, but something was missing. I just didn't feel right about going to bed with a stranger. I consider myself to be fairly liberated sexually but I guess I'm still a little old-fashioned. Nothing beats sex in a close, loving relationship."

It's impossible to change women so that they desire casual sex as much as men do. You certainly have a right to feel disappointed when your sexual desires go unmet. There's a difference between being frustrated and feeling resentful, however. It is important to realize that women's bodies are their own, not yours. They aren't under an obligation to meet your sexual needs. They have the right to say no for any reason, no matter how "sick" or "irrational" you may consider it to be. As a matter of fact, they have the right to say no and not even give a reason.

Be aware of the fear of pregnancy. You may easily forget a casual encounter, but a woman can receive an unwelcome reminder nine months later. Abortion is an option, but many women reject it on moral grounds. Even women who believe in abortion tend to go through a great deal of trauma from losing their unborn child. Fear of pregnancy is definitely not irrational.

A surprisingly high percentage of women are often ill-prepared for sex. The fear of cancer, nausea, gaining weight, etc. causes many sexually liberated women to avoid the birth control pill. Other forms of contraception are also unpopular with many women. Therefore, if a woman who is obviously attracted to you resists your advances, there is a high probability that she is not "protected" from pregnancy.

Some men, like boy scouts, are always prepared. They carry prophylactics in their wallets and quickly bring up the topic of contraception if they suspect it is the cause of a woman's reticence.

ERNIE: "I can't stand women who drink with me all night, screw me, and then kick me out. I'm terrified at the prospect of being arrested for drunken driving. I think it's very inconsiderate for a woman to subject me to the hazards of driving home after I've been drinking."

It certainly is inconsiderate. A similar problem arises if you smoke marijuana or use other drugs and are asked to leave while still under the influence. It would be nice if women would accept the responsibility for providing a man with the opportunity to stay until he is capable of driving safely. Unfortunately, not all women are so considerate. There are five things you can do to protect yourself:

1.  Drink moderately. Excessive alcohol is bad for your health and detracts from your sexual performance.
2.  Invite her to your home instead of going to hers.
3.  Call a taxi instead of driving home.
4.  Ask her to drive you home (if she isn't under the influence also).
5.  Be assertive and let her know that it isn't right for her to send you out on the road where you will be a hazard to yourself and others. Insist on staying until you are sober, either in her bedroom or on the sofa in the living room.

JOE: "I can't stand frigid women. I always feel like such a failure with them."

The Myth of the Frigid Woman is the counterpart to that of the Quick Shooter in the previous section. If you want to feel hostile towards a woman because she doesn't have an orgasm each time she makes love to you, that's your privilege. But you're not being very realistic. The fact is that the average American woman does not experience climax every time she has sexual intercourse.

Shere Hite discovered that 50% of women never have orgasms through intercourse. There are many reasons for this. One common explanation is that women are taught to hold back from men. Since men are often trying to seduce them, it is usually up to the woman to retain her composure

140

so that things don't get out of hand sexually. When women decide to say yes, they may find that subconsciously they are still holding back. It is then difficult for them to climax.

Complicating the issue of female orgasms is the fact that many women don't know if they have a climax during intercourse. This comes as a shock to most men since it is so obvious to them when they have an orgasm—they ejaculate. A woman's climax can be more subtle. Despite the descriptions in romantic novels and pornography, most female orgasms do not involve cannons exploding and bells ringing. A further problem is that there are at least two different types of female orgasm: vaginal and clitoral. A woman accustomed to climaxing through stimulation of her clitoris during masturbation or necking may not recognize the vaginal orgasm she experiences during intercourse.

Also contributing to the problem is the inability of many women to ask for what they want sexually. It would be far easier for a man to help his lover climax if he knew what turned her on sexually. Women are frequently afraid of being overly-erotic and explicit about their sexual needs and consequently miss out on the experience of orgasm.

Our attitudes toward sexuality in the "enlightened" twentieth century are in many ways as neurotic as those of the Victorian Era. The new hangup is performance. Men feel a great deal of pressure to be accomplished lovers and bring their partners to orgasm. Women feel equally pressured to be passionate and frequently feel compelled to fake orgasms. Pleasure gets lost in the shuffle.

JOHN: "Women are all freeloaders. They expect a man to pay for everything. It seems to me that if a lady is getting half the pleasure out of what we are doing, she should pay for half the freight."

Is this a legitimate gripe? Sally, a 37 year old divorcee, say no. "Women only earn 60% of what men get, thanks to discrimination, so it's only fair that men pick up the tab during dates." This is only a rationalization. Many women earn as much or more than the man and still refuse to pay their own way. Even in cases where they do earn less, they could at least offer to pay a proportion of the bill.

Another common reason given by women for not helping pay for dates is that the man may be offended or feel that she is "unladylike". This is certainly true with many men, particularly those over 40. They grew up before anyone had ever heard of women's liberation. Younger men, however, and many older ones as well, feel differently. Simenauer & Carroll discovered that three-quarters of men feel that women should occasionally either pay for the entire date or at least part of it.

Many women feel that men paying for dates is just one of the nice things about being a woman. They are naturally loathe to give up this privilege. Other women, however, prefer to pay their own way. Sally is a 37 year old apartment manager. "I always insist on paying for my share on a first date because I don't want to feel obliged to sleep with him just because he lays some bucks on me." Women who financially never pay for dates often wind up doing so sexually.

Regardless of whether or not women *should* help pay for dates, the fact is that they seldom do. This may not be fair, but it is reality. Men have several alternatives:

1.    You can pay and feel resentful.

2.    You can insist on women paying their own way on dates and refuse to date those who don't. If you do this, be prepared for hostility from women. Also realize that you will be eliminating the possibility of a romantic relationship with a large percentage of women.

3.    You can offer women a choice. Tell them you're prepared to pay but you also feel comfortable if they pay their own way.

4.    You can pay and not feel resentful. Be honest with yourself and admit if the shoe were on the other foot you probably would act the same way as women do. They are conditioned to expect men to pay and it is asking a great deal to require that they reject this conditioning. Also own up to the many economic advantages men have over women: the large salaries, greater career opportunities, easier credit, etc. Would you really be willing to give up these advantages for

true equality?

WILLIAM: "I resent girls who play hard to get. If I'm interested in someone, I make it real obvious. I wish girls would do the same."

Women do frequently play hard to get. Rather than feel angry, why not take it as a compliment? She may be afraid that she will lose you if she lets you know that she's crazy over you.

TOM: "Women are too emotional and irrational. They fall to pieces over the most insignificant things. Too often they rely on what they call intuition and what I call stupidity. Trying to reason with a woman is like beating your head against a wall!"

This is the flip side of the female resentment in the last section that men are insensitive and unable to express deep feeling. It's true that women tend to be more emotional than men. Far from being a negative quality, this is perhaps the most significant advantage of being a woman. Some women, of course, carry a good thing too far and are frequently incapable of controlling their feelings or thinking rationally. Sometimes they only pretend to lose control and break into tears as a means of manipulating a man.

The happy medium is to have the capacity to be either emotional or rational depending on whichever is most appropriate at the time. Men and women can learn a great deal from each other, but each needs to learn first to be more tolerant.

One secret for dealing with an overly-emotional woman (or man, for that matter) is to allow her to express her emotions thoroughly before trying to reason with her. When men or women are emotionally distraught, logic should be shelved until a more propitious moment.

ORVILLE: "Ladies worry too much about how much money a man makes. Just as they don't like to be treated as sex objects, we resent being money objects."

Despite women's liberation, many still have a "Cinderella Complex". They want a relationship with a man who "takes care of me". Resentment at being treated as an economic object is certainly legitimate. Unfortunately, it doesn't accomplish anything. Every man sadly has a choice: you can play the money-power-status game and be extremely attractive to a large portion of the female population or you can write them off and limit yourself to non-materialistic women.

BRUCE: "Ladies take forever to get ready. I can't stand waiting around all night while they put their faces on."

It is true that women usually take longer to get ready than men. A major reason for this, of course, is that most men are so demanding of women in terms of physical attractiveness. Women do not enjoy the many hours of hard work that go into looking beautiful. They do it to look good for men like you.

A woman has a right to take as long as she wishes to get ready. If she makes a commitment to you to be ready at a certain time, however, that's a different story. You have a right to be intolerant of broken commitments, as long as you didn't pressure her into making an unrealistic promise.

## EXERCISE

Play the VICTIM game described in the exercise on page 136. Choose a situation where a woman victimized you and you feel very resentful.

## A FINAL NOTE FOR MEN AND WOMEN

There is nothing wrong with having resentments. Don't deny or repress them. Be aware, however, that you have a choice about whether or not to hold on to them. Giving up resentments is not easy. The crucial first step is to drop the notion that other people are in this world to meet your expectations. They aren't. They're all too busy looking out for Number 1.

# DEALING WITH BAD HABITS

We are all creatures of habit. Most are beneficial, but a few can have devastating effects on your relationships. How you deal with them will play an important role in determining your romantic future. It's easy to feel resentful towards those who have bad habits you don't share. One way to get rid of these resentments is to face up to your own addictions. An addiction is anything you need daily and can't give up without discomfort. The most common are:

- smoking
- drinking
- caffeine (usually contained in coffee, tea and soft drinks)
- sugar
- sleeping pills
- cocaine
- downers
- marijuana
- food (addiction to food means eating more than your body requires)

What addictions do you have? If you honestly believe you have no addictions, take the following test. For one week, quit using any of the above items you ingest daily. If you wind up feeling nervous, depressed or developing headaches, you're addicted, whether you want to admit it or not.

Being holier than thou feels great but it gets in the way of making romantic contact. Learn to be more tolerant of the problems and addictions of others. As Jesus said, don't tell your neighbor about the splinter in his eye when you fail to notice the beam in your own.

## SMOKING

If you are a non-smoker, you must decide whether or not to tolerate smoking by others. If you are willing to immediately eliminate one-third of your chances for meeting someone special, then your choice is simple: don't date smokers. If you aren't willing to do this, consider the following options:

1.  Allow people to smoke in your presence any time and any place. This is the ideal attitude, as long as you find it easy to tolerate smoke.

2.  Allow people to smoke in your home but insist that they do so away from you. For example, the other side of the room, in a different room or outdoors on the patio.

3.  Allow people to smoke in your presence, but not under the following circumstances:
    *   in a confined space or place with poor ventiliation
    *   in front of your children
    *   in your own home

4.  Demand that they quit. This rarely works. Smoking is an addiction. Otherwise, millions of Americans wouldn't fail to quit each year.

Once you have decided if and under what circumstances you will tolerate smoking, make your wishes known in an honest but friendly manner. Smokers can then take you or leave you. Another possibility is to work out a compromise which enables them to smoke but doesn't cause severe discomfort for you.

Many non-smokers go off the deep end about smoking. Granted there is some evidence that being around smokers can be hazardous to your health. The danger is probably minimal, however, unless people are blowing smoke in your face all day long. Occasionally being around smokers is not going to be severely detrimental.

146

Some people, of course, have emphysema or other ailments which require them to avoid smoke. Others are severely allergic. It is proper that they limit their romantic relationships to people who either don't smoke or will abstain in their presence.

Many people who claim that "smoke makes me sick" are lying to themselves, however. Tom is a 42 year old art dealer. "I have never smoked but for many years hardly noticed if others lit up. After all the negative publicity came out about smoking, however, I started to pay more attention and developed a resentful attitude towards smokers. I found that the more resentment I felt, the more sensitive I became to the effects of smoke. Obviously a major cause of my discomfort was mental rather than physical."

What do you do if the shoe is on the other foot: you're the smoker? The best thing to do, of course, is quit. If you are unwilling or unable to do so, bear in mind the following suggestions:

1.  Be aware of how offensive smoking can be to non-smokers.

2.  Obey non-smoking signs in stores, banks, etc.

3.  As much as possible, try to smoke either alone or with other smokers.

4.  Don't be afraid to go into another room or step outside to smoke when you are among non-smokers.

5.  Ask for permission to smoke. Caution: be aware of the risk you are taking if you do this. If they answer no, you are stuck with not smoking. Don't be a jerk and ask, "Mind if I smoke?" and then get angry if the person says, "Yes, I do mind."

6.  Discuss your smoking habit with non-smokers and see if you can work out an agreement that meets both their needs and yours.

Following the suggestions above will enable you to get along well with the non-smoking majority and possibly find a non-smoker for a romantic relationship.

## DRINKING

Numerous women are terrified of getting involved with a man with a drinking problem. These women usually come from a home where the father was an alcoholic. Either that or they suffered the misfortune of having married one.

Alcohol is one of the most severe problems that can affect a romantic relationship. Alcoholics have a strong tendency to be violent with their lovers, wives or children. Almost every arena of performance, from the office to the bedroom, is adversely affected by excess booze.

The safest course is to avoid getting involved with anyone who drinks. Unfortunately, this means eliminating the overwhelming majority of single people in this country. Furthermore, just because a person doesn't drink in your presence doesn't mean that he abstains all the time. Even if he is "on the wagon" when you meet him, that doesn't insure that he won't fall into a drunken binge next month.

What can you do to avoid involvement with an alcoholic? The following advice is from a woman's perspective, since they tend to be the most fearful. However, men should also be concerned about falling in love with an alcoholic. Watch carefully for signs of alcoholism. They aren't always easy to spot. An alcoholic or problem drinker doesn't always collapse in a drunken stupor. Many otherwise successful men go to great lengths to conceal their problem with alcohol. The signs to watch for are:

1. Does he drink every day? (Exclude a glass or two or wine at meals, which is the custom in many families.)

2. Does he go through pronounced emotional change after he drinks? The average person loses some inhibitions and becomes more cheerful and even silly when he drinks, but an alcoholic may become angry, depressed or even violent after drinking.

3. Does he find it difficult to stop once he starts drinking? Does he have to finish the bottle?

Some less conclusive indicators of a potential problem with

alcohol are:

1. Does he drink alone?
2. Does he drink in the morning?
3. Does he drink one particular type of mixed drink almost to the exclusion of all others?

What do you do if you're involved with an alcoholic? If you are reasonably sure about this, you have several options:

1. Dump him. This may sound cruel but why ruin your life just to share his misery?

2. Insist that he change. This is a weak option because people seldom make radical changes to please someone. An alcoholic will usually respond to your demand in one of the following ways:

   - He will deny that he is an alcoholic. He may even be "sincere" in the sense that he isn't lying to you—he's deceiving himself. Unless he admits that he is an alcoholic, he will not change.
   - He will admit that he has a "slight drinking problem" but is not an alcoholic. Again, as long as he adheres to this position, he will not change.
   - He will admit that he has a serious problem and promise to change. This is very positive but promises are often easy to make and difficult to keep. This is particularly true in the case of alcoholics who are often talented con-artists with their loved ones. The only thing you can really trust is deeds, not words.
   - He will become involved with an alcohol treatment program or join an organization such as Alcoholics Anonymous. Here at least there is good reason for hope. There are millions of reformed alcoholics in this country. If a person sincerely embarks on a reform program and appears to be making good progress, he may be worth the gamble. Be aware, however, of the grievous price you will pay if the gamble doesn't work out.

149

The overwhelming majority of men in this country are not alcoholics, so why play with fire? The safe course is to avoid them unless they admit they have a problem and are working hard to overcome it. They then may be safer bets than those who are not yet alcoholics but are on their way.

What if you're not sure that someone is an alcoholic? There are several things you can do to resolve the question.

1.   Study alcoholism. Your local church, library, hospital, physician or alcohol treatment center will have pamphlets and books dealing with this subject. Armed with this information, you can make a more valid diagnosis.

2.   Ask an expert. Describe the symptoms and ask for a diagnosis.

3.   Ask the man's ex-wives/girlfriends, relatives, neighbors, friends, or business associates. This is a risky suggestion, since he will probably become quite angry if he finds out you have been spying on him. However, if you suspect him of alcoholism but don't have conclusive evidence, this may be the only way of making an intelligent decision.

## COCAINE

Cocaine is the headline-grabbing drug of the Eighties. So long as it is used recreationally (once a week or less), you shouldn't have any problem relating to a cocaine user (unless you're paying for it). Unfortunately, more frequent use can change a person's outlook on life. Abusers of cocaine lose interest in their jobs, lovers, family and friends. They become obsessed with the drug. They can become unreliable, irritable and brusque. They frequently lie about where they are going to cover their drug use. They can also become dependent on coke in order to have sex. Financially the abuse of cocaine is a disaster, since it is extremely expensive. If you date someone who uses cocaine, find out whether it's recreational. If you learn that a person is a frequent user, you would be wise to find someone else for a romantic relationship.

## DOWNERS
There are three major categories of these drugs:
- minor tranquilizers, such as valium or librium
- sedative hypnotics, such as quaaludes ("ludes") or seconal ("reds")
- pain-killers, such as codeine or darvon

It's difficult to condemn downer abuse if you understand the usual cause: medical problems. Many people were originally prescribed these drugs by their physicians to deal with nervousness, sleep difficulties and physical pain. Unfortunately, they are highly addictive and cause personality changes. If a person has developed a dependency on downers after a recent medical problem, there may not be that much cause for alarm. On the other hand, if abuse of these drugs goes on for years and becomes a major part of a person's lifestyle (running around to three or four different physicians to get prescriptions), consider finding someone else.

## MARIJUANA
In comparison with the preceding drugs, marijuana is relatively benign. Problems can arise, however, with daily use. If you want to be involved with someone ambitious and dynamic, stay away from heavy users. "Pot heads" tend to lay around the house and do nothing. Some develop an "Annie Hall" syndrome, where they need to smoke marijuana before sex in order to face the anxiety of intimacy.

## A FINAL WORD ON HABITS
Bad habits put a heavy strain on relationships. Rather than feel resentful, the wisest course is to avoid people who have habits you find intolerable. Be aware, however, of the price you pay each time you write off people with a particular habit: you are shrinking the number of people available for a loving relationship with you.

151

# PREJUDICES AND STEREOTYPES

In addition to people with "bad habits," you may have a tendency to exclude other categories of people because of misinformation or negative conditioning. This is tragic, not only for them but also for you. Each group of people that you eliminate reduces your chances of finding the right person for a romantic relationship. It is crucial, therefore, to discover your prejudices and stereotypes and try to overcome them.

## AGE PREJUDICE
Men and women are both victimized by age prejudice. A good example is older women. Men have been brainwashed to believe that younger women are more attractive than those that are older and particularly that women over 40 are "over the hill". What are the facts?

It is generally true that younger women have slimmer, more athletic bodies, fewer wrinkles, more lustrous hair and are less likely to have stretch marks. Nature does compensate, however, as Brian discovered. "Like most guys, my fantasy lady is young, slim and gorgeous. My problem is that I find most younger women to be empty-headed. I have a hard time carrying on a conversation with them—there are a lot of blank spots when I run out of things to say and she's having the same problem. I find that I prefer talking to older women. They're usually not as beautiful (although I've met some dynamite women in their 40s) but they're a lot more interesting. So I'm torn between lusting after the young stuff and actually connecting more easily with older women."

On the level of compatibility, there is a lot to be said for younger men dating older women. After 16, men begin to go downhill sexually, while women reach their peak sexually around age 40. Tim is a 19 year old anthropology student at a university. "I met Claudia in the classroom—she was the professor. I really didn't notice her that much at first. Sure, she was attractive. Some of the guys in the class would joke about how they wouldn't mind a "private lesson" with her. But I figured that she had to be at least 40 (actually she was 39) and I wasn't looking for a surrogate mother.

"As the semester went on, I found myself liking her more and more. Claudia was superb at leading discussions. She knew how to draw out all of her students and get them to open up—including the shy ones like myself. At the end of the semester, we had a class party in her home. I had a little too much to drink and wound up sleeping it off on her couch. The next morning she cooked us a great breakfast and we started to talk. Before I knew it, I was telling her my life story. She really listened. She was the first person I ever met who really wanted to hear the whole thing—all the silly things as well as the high points.

"We didn't do anything sexually that day—I was too shy and I guess she was a little paranoid about her job. We started getting together regularly after that, though, and became lovers. I expected her to be a little tame sexually. Was I surprised! She was a tigress in bed. I had only slept with a few girls before—all teenagers. They gave me the impression they were doing me a favor. Claudia didn't have that attitude at all. She called me her young stallion and taxed me to my limits. I've had other girlfriends since Claudia, but all in my own age group. None of them has been as passionate or interesting to be with. I learned a lot from Claudia and it wasn't all anthropology."

Many women lie about their age or refuse to discuss the question altogether because of the incredible prejudice they encounter. It's incredible, because when you come right down to it a woman is either attractive or not. If you find out her age, it isn't going to make her prettier or uglier. It won't remove any wrinkles or make her more interesting. If "a rose by any other name would smell as sweet," then a

153

woman of any other age would still be as attractive.

For those women who are contemptuous of men because of their age prejudice, it is a shock to realize that women are far more prejudiced about age than men. When I first started working with a dating club, I was very surprised by the number of times handsome men in their 20s would select women in their 30s for a date and be rejected. I would have guessed that the women would be flattered. The almost universal response was, "I don't go out with babies."

I can recall asking a woman named Lillian out for a date. She was 8 or 9 years older than I but I found her attractive. She was supposed to come over to my home for dinner but cancelled the night before—something about not being able to get a baby sitter. Later we became platonic friends and I found out that the babysitting problem was just an excuse. She didn't feel comfortable going out with a man so much younger than she. The story has an interesting conclusion. Years later she wound up dating steadily a man even younger than I.

Older men have a mystique for women. Some have suggested that it goes back to Freud's "Electra complex" where little girls were attracted to their fathers. Whatever the reason, many women are terribly prejudiced against younger men. The wrinkles that men find so distasteful are "signs of character" to many women. The grey hair which is anathema on a female head looks "distinguished" on a man.

The irony is that male and female age prejudices are completely opposite to what they should be from the viewpoint of longevity. Women on the average outlive men by as much as 7 years. What that means is that a woman who marries a man 2 to 3 years older than she is asking to be a widow for 9 to 10 years. When I am a guest on radio talk shows, I frequently suggest to women that they marry men as much as seven years younger than they. They think I'm crazy. Personally I believe they are the ones who are insane if they refuse to date younger men.

Karen, a long-time friend, was 60 when she underwent the severe trauma of her husband dying. After so many years of marriage, she found she couldn't adjust to living alone and tried to find another man. Square dancing turned out to be ideal for her needs—she enjoyed it and also met several men to date.

All of the men were older than she. Several proposed marriage. Always the kibitzer, I asked her why she wanted to marry these older men and open herself up to the strong probability of again experiencing the tragedy of widowhood. Why not date younger men? Karen wouldn't hear of it—why would a younger man date an old bag when there were so many younger women to choose from? I told her that she was slim, pretty and dressed beautifully and, therefore, didn't have to settle for an older man. When she was 63 she met a 52 year old civil servant. A few months later they were man and wife.

The result of age prejudice is that men under 35 and women over 40 are in trouble. There are more boys than girls born each year and, therefore, more single men than women until age 35. By that time, enough men have died and there are equal numbers of single men and women. Since many women under 35 are dating older men, a large surplus of young men are left out. Later the tables are reversed. Due to superior longevity, by the time a woman reaches age 55, there are 2½ women for every single man of that age. Since many of these men are dating women in their 40s (and even younger), the pickings are very slim for most middle-aged and elderly women.

This great American tragedy of young men and older women being left in the cold can be averted only if we break through the senseless age prejudices we have. All of the prejudices and stereotypes in this chapter take a heavy toll in preventing romances.

## RACIAL PREJUDICE

We live in a racist society, so naturally most Americans are prejudiced against people of other races. Consider the consequences: if you are prejudiced against black people, you may be crossing 11% of the population off your list of prospects—regardless of their physical beauty, wealth, intelligence, sense of humor, etc. If you are prejudiced against Asians or Chicanos or other minority groups, you are eliminating millions more. If you are biased against Caucasians instead, you are crossing off the vast majority of prospects in the United States.

Certainly there are many disadvantages to dating

people of other races. Just remember that you do have a choice. You have the right to date people of racial heritages and nationalities other than your own. Beauty, talent and goodness are not limited to any one group of people.

If you find people of other nationalities and races to be unattractive, then by all means don't date them. Don't make the mistake of dating minorities to prove you aren't racist.

Stereotypes are often a cause of racial prejudice. Some examples are:

"Mexicans are lazy."

"Japanese are treacherous"

"Blacks are only good at sports, dancing and entertainment."

These stereotypes are certainly true in some cases. What makes them dangerous is that people tend to think that *all* members of a particular group share these characteristics, which is not true. If you allow yourself to believe these stereotypes, you are likely to miss out on the opportunity to become friends with some very special individuals.

## RELIGIOUS PREJUDICE

It has been said that more people have died in religious wars than any other type of conflict. Many potential loving relationships have also died or failed to materialize because of religious differences. There was a time when Catholics only married Catholics. Protestants and Jews were equally intolerant of other religions. Fortunately, religious prejudice has greatly diminished in recent decades but it still exists.

Have you ever *not* dated someone because of their religion? If so, consider the price you pay for your religious prejudice. If you are biased against Jews, for example, you are depriving yourself of millions of prospects for a romantic relationship. Likewise, if you won't date Mormons, Witnesses of Jehovah, Baptists, Catholics, etc.

Almost every religion claims to be the "one true religion." Nobody has ever been able to prove it, however. The fact is that there are numerous geniuses who belong to every church you can think of and there also are many brilliant people who are atheists. Under those circumstances, it is unwise to be prejudiced against other religions.

If your religious affiliation is crucial to you, it may be foolish to date people of other churches. Otherwise, try dating people of other faiths. You may fall in love with one of them.

## SOCIO-ECONOMIC PREJUDICE

America is not as class-conscious as many other countries (such as England or India), but socio-economic prejudice is still common here. If you are prejudiced against people whose ancestors didn't come over on the Mayflower or aren't millionaires, you are eliminating over 200 million people. If you are only prejudiced against poor people, you are still missing out on many millions of prospects.

## EDUCATIONAL PREJUDICE

There was a time when a high school diploma was a status symbol. Today even Masters Degrees are becoming a dime a dozen. Millions of young Americans are on an educational treadmill where they sacrifice years of their lives and many thousands of dollars to earn what frequently is a useless degree in terms of future employment. One thing the degree does confer, however, is status. Woe to those who don't have the right diploma—they are ostracized into the ranks of the ignorant!

Truly educated people know that there isn't necessarily a correlation between formal education and either knowledge or intelligence. Too often, however, intelligent, self-educated people are rejected as unworthy of others with the proper pedigree.

There is nothing foolish about wanting to be involved with people who are on an intellectual level similar to your own—this enhances communication and compatibility. To reject someone because they didn't attend the right school or earn the proper degree, however, is ridiculous.

## DIVORCE PREJUDICE

Many people are prejudiced against divorced people. The stereotype is that they're all losers who drove their spouses away because of their defects of character or personality. Those who have never married are particularly prone to believe this stereotype and avoid dating divorced people, but so, too, are the divorced themselves. Guy is a 38 year old who has never been married. "I never date divorcees. I figure if they couldn't hold on to their husbands, there must be something wrong with them. I've never married because my parents were divorced and I want to make sure that if I get married, it's for life. I don't want to take any chances with a woman with a poor track record."

This is all nonsense. Survey studies reveal that people who remarry are just as happy as people who are still in a first marriage. There is no reason to believe a second marriage won't be successful. Fortunately, despite the prejudice against divorced people, five-sixths of divorced men and three-quarters of divorced women remarry, according to Robert Weiss in his book *Marital Separation.*

## FIRST IMPRESSIONS

Perhaps the most widespread and unfair of all prejudices and stereotypes are those we develop on the basis of first impressions. It's easy to pre-judge people on the basis of very limited information: the clothes they wear, hairstyles, a facial expression, the sound of their voices. Here are some examples of how first impressions can lead you astray.

1. A man is dressed in old jeans and tennis shoes. You conclude he is poor. In reality, he may be a prosperous businessman who is tired of wearing $500 suits all the time and prefers old, comfortable clothes during his leisure time.

2. A woman is wearing a revealing blouse. You decide that she is promiscuous. In reality, she is quite strait-laced but decided to wear the blouse in order to attract attention.

3. A man is smiling frequently, so you conclude that he is a happy, friendly person. The truth is that he is chronically depressed but feeling good today because he just got hired for a new job.

4.   A woman is frowning and looking sad. You write her off as a miserable loser. The fact is that she is normally cheerful but recently received news about a death in the family.

Inevitably you will make snap judgments and categorize people. The important thing is that you be willing to change your stereotypes about people as you learn new information about them. Even a lifetime would be insufficient to learn everything about a person, so don't ever conclude that you have "their number"—people are full of surprises.

**EXERCISE**
1.   Pay attention to the quick judgments you make about the next five people you meet.

2.   Check out these judgments with them. For example, "You seem to be very shy; are you?" or "I get the impression that you're the nervous type" or "You seem to be very conservative" or "You appear to be the happiest person in the room."

You will probably discover you are right some of the time but dead wrong a good deal, also. Hopefully, you will learn to be less certain about your first impressions and be open to discovering who people really are.

# LOOKING GOOD

We have seen how important first impressions are. This is particularly true about your physical appearance. When someone attractive comes along, it's important that he or she be immediately attracted to you physically. Otherwise there is a low probability of a romantic relationship.

Five percent of the population are lucky enough to have been born beautiful. The rest of us have to work at it. Let's begin with the physique or figure. Americans are obsessed with slimness, despite medical data that suggest that our weight charts may be all wrong. Ideal weights may be significantly higher than was previously thought. Regardless of the scientific controversy, the fact is that fat is not considered attractive by most people.

So what do you do if you're fat? Obviously there are two ways to lose weight: Increase the number of calories you burn or decrease your intake of food. Exercise is, therefore, one key to weight loss. If you're like most Americans, you're probably quite sedentary and do very little vigorous exercise. Discover a sport or physical activity that you can enjoy. We are fortunate in this country to have thousands of volleyball, tennis, basketball and racquetball courts. There are jogging tracks and weightlifting equipment, bicycles and exercise machines, swimming pools, golf courses, and baseball fields. Hopefully you can enjoy one or more of the many athletic alternatives.

Dancing is a great form of exercise. Ballroom, disco, rock, Latin, folk and square dancing are all great for losing weight. Walking is excellent, also. Try leaving your car at home and walking to work, the store or friends' homes.

One advantage of developing an exercise program is that it can coincide with your goal of meeting people. To paraphrase advice from a previous chapter, find out where the ducks are exercising and join them. Hopefully you will be losing weight *and* meeting prospects.

Unfortunately, exercise is usually not enough. Most overweight people inevitably face the need for dieting. Some studies claim that as many as 98% of people who go on a diet either fail to lose a significant amount of weight or regain it later. The problem seems to be that people go from one extreme to another. They diet and then binge. There appears to be almost universal agreement among the experts that what works is to avoid crash diets and permanently alter your eating habits instead.

This may require behavior modification counseling (ask your physician to refer you to a therapist with the proper credentials) or choosing a diet you can live with— for the rest of your life.

It's possible to have an ideal weight (according to the charts) and still be flabby. It's also possible to weigh more than the "ideal" and still be in excellent physical condition. The difference is muscle tone. Even if dieting is a dead-end, you can still develop good muscle tone. Beginning a vigorous exercise program, as suggested above, is one way of achieving this. So are fitness centers, athletic clubs, or doing calisthenics at home. There are numerous books, tapes, records and television programs on physical fitness. Take advantage of them.

## TANS

As in the case of weight, we Americans have an irrational view of proper skin care. Any dermatologist will tell you the sun is dangerous: millions of Americans suffer from skin cancer. Also, the sun dries out the skin, causing wrinkles and freckles. Medically, the wise course is to minimize your exposure to the sun.

Unfortunately, the wise course is not always the popular one. If you want to be attractive to the opposite sex, a Coppertone tan can be an important advantage. If you have the time and inclination (and your skin isn't the kind that only burns and never tans), lie out in the sun as often as possible. (Incidentally, beaches and swimming pools are also great for meeting people.) If you don't have the time or it's winter, consider going to a tanning parlor. Take care to use a good sunscreen. Suntan lotions all list a protection factor. Anything under a 4 is too low, unless you already have a good tan protecting you.

## GLASSES

Most people find eyeglasses to be unattractive, so avoid them if possible. Contact lenses are an important option to consider, particularly for women. Unfortunately, eyeglasses give women a school marm image, which most men don't find sexy. A man can more easily get away with wearing glasses. They make him look more intelligent, dignified and professorial, which many women find attractive.

Some people insist on wearing sunglasses in order to look "cool". Often they just look silly or cover their eyes, which may be their best feature. Sunglasses also get in the way of good eye contact, which is crucial for communication. So avoid sunglasses except to protect your eyes from the sun.

## PERSONAL HYGIENE

This is another area of American irrationality. Smelling good is not crucial to good health, but it can be essential to being attractive. Bathing, using a deodorant, brushing and flossing your teeth, and even using breath mints should be daily activities when you're hunting ducks.

Taking good care of your teeth will also add to your visual attractiveness. Extremely crooked or "buck" teeth can be a major liability. Perfect teeth are not a necessity, but if you are cursed with really ugly teeth, consider visiting an orthodontist. Orthodontia is not just for kids.

Arlene is a 24 year old secretary. "I used to have quite a complex about my teeth. They were so awful looking I was ashamed to smile. I kept myself under tight control lest I open my mouth and display my deformity. And, of course, I was too shy to flirt with anybody.

"My parents talked about getting braces for me when I was growing up but there never was enough money. Finally, after graduating from high school, I decided to save up the money myself. It took me three years but I finally went out and got my teeth fixed. It looked ridiculous for a woman in her twenties to be a "metal mouth," but I figured that I didn't have much to lose—I already was ashamed of my looks. Now my teeth are almost perfect and I have a beautiful smile (or at least that's what the guys tell me). I've come out of my shell and have no trouble meeting men."

## COLOGNE AND PERFUME

Most men are attracted to women who wear perfume; likewise most women prefer a man who wears a good aftershave or cologne. If you're allergic or uncomfortable wearing scents, then don't. They aren't crucial. They can be a valuable asset, however, when you are around attractive people of the opposite sex. It's important, of course, to choose a pleasant scent that is appropriate for you. Try different perfumes or colognes and ask your friends of the opposite sex for their opinions. If you can't get honest feedback from your friends, then try strangers. ("Do you like the smell of my perfume/aftershave?" is a good opening line, by the way.)

## PLASTIC SURGERY

If you have plenty of money and don't like one or more features of your face or neck, consider plastic surgery. It can reduce lines and wrinkles, cover up scars, change the shape of your nose, etc. Any aging movie star can tell you that it does work.

## JEWELRY

Men, in particular, are usually attracted by jewelry, but women also frequently express a preference for men who wear tasteful, non-gaudy jewelry. If you enjoy and can afford jewelry, then by all means go ahead and wear it. If not, skip it. It's not that important.

## CLOTHES

They say that "clothes make the man." This can be true for women as well. If you have an attractive body, clothes can enhance it; if your body is unattractive, you can literally cover up this fact with a good wardrobe.

The first requirement is that your clothes be clean and

sweet-smelling. Avoid clothes that are too old or frayed. It's also important that they be well-tailored. Baggy clothes are not sexy. Wearing "floods" (clothes with sleeves or legs that are too short) is considered contemptible except during typhoons.

The shape and attractiveness of your body should determine your wardrobe. A slim (but not skinny) body suggests tight clothes to show it off. Fat people should be wary of tight clothes.

Color coordination is crucial. We have all seen people who look like clowns because they wear too many colors or choose those that clash. It's important that your tops, bottoms, shoes, scarves, ties, overcoats, furs and jewelry match. If you have poor taste or are color blind, the safest thing is to buy suits and ask the salesperson to choose matching ties, scarves, shirts, blouses, shoes or other accessories for you. Better still, if you have a friend or relative who has good taste, ask them to go shopping with you. If you can afford it, hire a wardrobe consultant to go shopping with you. A cheaper alternative is to buy a book on proper dress. John T. Molloy has written two excellent books on the subject: *Dress For Success* (for men) and *The Women's Dress For Success Book*. The emphasis in both books is on dressing professionally, but there are chapters on looking good for the opposite sex as well. Due to my own notorious bad taste in clothes, I was forced to buy Molloy's book *and* ask a friend to go shopping with me.

### FABRICS

Natural fibers (like cotton) are more expensive than synthetics (such as dacron) and also require more ironing. Unfortunately, they also are more attractive to the opposite sex. Particularly if you're a man, concern yourself with fabrics since women have a tendency to choose men who dress in a way that indicates success and wealth. Polyester is out.

### TIPS FOR WOMEN

### DRESSING SEXY

There are three main things about a woman's apparel that turn on a man sexually:

164

1.  that the clothes look attractive on her
2.  that the clothes be tight
3.  that as much skin as possible be revealed.

A woman can be sexy by wearing attractive clothes that aren't tight or revealing, but it's more difficult. Tight clothes have disadvantages, of course. They can be very uncomfortable. They also show off imperfections as well as attractive curves.

How much skin to reveal can be a tricky question. There is a fine line between being sexy and looking cheap. Men love to see almost any part of the female anatomy. Bikinis, shorts, backless evening gowns, short skirts, halters, and tank tops are all favorites of men. Going without a bra can be very sexy. Just be sure you have the figure to allow this.

John T. Molloy did extensive research on what men find sexy in women. In his aforementioned *Women's Dress For Success Book*, he reports the following findings:

1.  Don't ever be among the first to buy a fashion—you run the risk of losing your investment if it doesn't catch on.
2.  Wear pants if you are neither extremely large nor extra thin.
3.  Wear tight sweaters made of soft wool or cashmere.
4.  Wear tight vests. The color of the vest should contrast with that of the suit.
5.  Only wear skin-colored pantyhose. The other colors do not attract men.
6.  Wear tight gloves.
7.  Don't streak or frost your hair.
8.  Wear minimum makeup, unless you are over 45 and have wrinkles to hide.
9.  Wear delicate and expensive perfume.
10. Don't wear sunglasses. Don't wear designer glasses either—they make you look heavier.
11. Instead of spreading your money out to buy a lot of cheap jewelry, save up for one or more exquisite pieces.
12. Try to contrast the colors of your lingerie or swimsuits with your own skin color. For example, if you

165

have very light skin, wear black or bright red. If you have a good tan, wear a white bathing suit. In general, both black and white women look best in red lingerie. The second best color for white women is black; for black women, it's pale pink. Skin tones, grey and teal blue are not sexy to men. Men love variety, so if you have a steady boyfriend or husband, wear different colors of lingerie.

13. Wear lace, particularly if there is a "peekaboo" element to it. Also wear frilly clothing.
14. Only wear a two-piece swimsuit if you have a good figure. Otherwise, wear a one-piece.

Don't be surprised if men come on to you or get gross when you dress sexy. You can't have your cake and eat it, too. If you dress provocatively, men will respond accordingly.

## DRESSING ELEGANTLY
You may discover that dressing sexy attracts the wrong type of man. Consider the alternative of being elegant. Dressing this way will certainly attract male attention. A cultured, refined, wealthy man may overlook the woman who dresses sexy in favor of one more elegant.

On the other hand, you may scare away some men who worry that you have "too much class". You may also stand out like a sore thumb if you are the only person dressed elegantly. The safe course is to strike a happy medium, being part elegant and part sexy. That will enable you to attract plenty of men.

## DYEING YOUR HAIR
As was pointed out in the chapter on Prejudices and Stereotypes, the vast majority of American men insist on dating a youthful woman. Grey hair can definitely put a damper on your dating, particularly if it is premature. Some women have beautiful white hair that is quite becoming, but they are the exception.

There is good reason to doubt the efficacy of dyeing your hair blond. Despite the cliche that blonds have more fun, there is evidence from surveys that brunettes are just as popular with men. Possibly makeout artists looking for an easy score prefer blonds, since they have an image of being looser sexually. The man looking for more than a one night stand, however, is probably not going to discriminate against brunettes. The waste of time, money and energy (plus the possible damage to your hair) are not balanced by the dubious advantage of being a blond.

Many men make contemptuous remarks about "bleached blonds". If you dye your hair, be religious about touching up the roots. Also be prepared for possible disappointment on a man's part when he discovers that you're not a natural blond.

## LENGTH OF HAIR

Dian Hanson, in her book, *How To Pick Up Men*, states that 80% of the men she interviewed preferred long hair. Only a small percentage of men prefer short hair. Many consider long, flowing locks to be a woman's glory. Short hair can definitely lower your datability. Hair that is particularly short also leads to being labeled as a lesbian.

Of course, many women have important reasons for keeping their hair short. Long hair requires a great deal of maintenance. Athletic women, in particular, find it to be a terrible inconvenience. Women in the business world usually prefer shorter hair because it gives them a more professional image. Many women also find that short hair is more flattering to their bone structure. Despite all the disadvantages, however, give serious consideration to wearing your hair at least to shoulder or near-shoulder length.

## FACIAL AND BODY HAIR

Mustaches are considered sexy on a man. Alas, this isn't true for women. Any woman with dark or thick facial hair should consider electrolysis. Shaving legs and armpits is also vital, unless the hair is unnoticeable due to fineness or light color. The natural look of hairy armpits and legs is favored by only a small minority of men.

## MAKEUP

Many men are adamant against heavy makeup (or any makeup at all) and prefer a more natural look. Certainly thick makeup can be rather comical and reminiscent of teeny boppers trying to look glamorous. Nevertheless, most men favor tasteful makeup. It can greatly enhance the beauty of your eyes and lips, cover blemishes, scars and imperfections, and give your skin a vibrant color. If you are not adept at makeup, sign up for one of the many inexpensive beauty seminars and classes available in most communities.

## PAINTED NAILS
Most men find women to be more elegant and attractive if they have painted nails.

## THE IDEAL WOMAN
For many years, the American ideal was a big-breasted, voluptuous woman like Marilyn Monroe, Jayne Mansfield and Raquel Welch. Standards of beauty constantly change, however, and the slender, well-muscled, athletic look is now "in".

In past decades, women who did not have the right curves either developed inferiority complexes or wore "falsies". Later medical technology was tapped to provide breast implants to supplement what nature had provided. One of the blessings of the new athletic look is that theoretically, any woman can meet the ideal if she is willing to sweat long enough.

If you're a buxom, rubenesque type woman and hate exercise, don't panic. There are still millions of men who like curves and prefer the Dolly Parton look. On the other hand, if you have a slender, boyish figure, all you have to do is develop a few muscles and you'll be chic.

Don't make the mistake of comparing yourself with playmates in the men's magazines. As Dian Hanson points out, these women are just fantasy objects for men. They'd "rather stroke your warm, soft, smaller breast than watch Loni Anderson's juggle across a television soundstage a thousand miles away."

## TIPS FOR MEN

## BALDNESS
Thinning hair or baldness need not be catastrophic. Bald men have a mystique of being more sexy and virile. Lack of hair certainly hasn't hurt the sex appeal of Yul Brynner or Telly Savalas. Of course, if you want to project

a youthful image, hair is a must. Otherwise, if you have thinning hair, you can still be attractive to most women.

The crucial thing is your own attitude. If baldness wreaks havoc on your self-confidence and makes you feel unattractive to women then do something about it. Consider wearing a hairpiece or investigate hair-weaving and hair transplants. The problem with hairpieces is that observant people often can pick them out. Be leery of claims that a particular wig is totally undetectable. Hair transplants look better but can be quite expensive. The one thing you should never do is purchase any of the "cures" for baldness. They are all rip-offs, without exception.

## HAIR

Unlike women, men look distinguished in grey hair. You don't need to dye your hair unless you seek a more youthful image. Length of hair is not critical as long as extremes are avoided. Very long hair or crewcuts are unattractive to most women. It's important to keep abreast of the latest styles and wear your hair accordingly. A good hair stylist is highly recommended. Molloy found that most women were "completely turned off by men with dirty (or even dirty-looking) hair."

Beards and mustaches are considered masculine and, therefore, desirable by many women. On the other hand, the clean-cut look is also very popular. Choose whichever looks most attractive on you. Often a weak chin, scars, blemishes, or other unpleasant features can be concealed by a beard or mustache. There are many unattractive clean-shaven men who are quite handsome with a beard. Molloy's research reveals that mustaches are particularly attractive to women.

Be careful, however, not to grow a scraggly beard or sparse mustache. They look ridiculous and turn women off. Growing a beard or mustache to look older can be an effective tactic, but make sure that you don't remind people of a teenager trying to conceal his callow age.

## MUSCLES

Surveys claim that American women prefer tall, slim men. I have heard numerous women claim that they are not attracted to guys who are muscle-bound. I don't believe them. I've seen enough women swoon over muscles to believe that the Arnold Schwarznegger look is definitely "in". Scrawny is "out".

Fortunately, there are numerous fitness centers, gyms, and health clubs throughout the country that feature body-building equipment and programs. If you look like a guy in the Charles Atlas ads who gets sand kicked in his face, you might consider doing something to build up your musculature.

## FORMAL DRESS

Many women are favorably impressed by men who wear a coat and tie. It's a sign of wealth and success. Of course, there is also the possibility of the woman you are trying to impress finding you to be stuffy. You can't please everyone.

Be careful not to overdress; a coat and tie are not appropriate at a pool party. Be just as careful not to be casually attired at a formal dinner party. Specific circumstances should dictate how you dress. Ask yourself, how will everyone else be dressed? While being a non-conformist will certainly gain attention, it's also likely to get you rejected.

## WARDROBE

Traditionally, women have been far more knowledgeable about clothes than men. Don Juan, the legendary lover, advised letting a woman pick out your clothing. Molloy suggests that most women would be flattered to have you ask her to help you choose garments that look sexy on you.

It's important to dress well for two reasons: 1) you will be more attractive to women; 2) according to Molloy, woman judge your intelligence by how you dress. If you dress stupidly (your clothes fit poorly, don't match, or accentuate your worse physical features), she may conclude that you are stupid. Since intelligence and physical attractiveness are high on the list of qualities women prefer in their men, you will have two strikes against you before you even say hello if you're a poor dresser.

## TEN COMMANDMENTS
1.   Wear clothes that make you *feel* attractive.
2.   Wear tight clothes if you are not overweight. Women

find them sexy.

3. Wear loose (but not baggy) clothes if you're over-weight.

4. Never wear white socks unless you're wearing tennis shoes. They have the same effect as wearing a bright neon sign that reads, "Nerd".

5. If you understand color coordination, contrast your colors. Women are attracted to men who dress cleverly.

6. If you don't understand color coordination, play it safe and wear clothes that you know match. Since most men don't understand color coordination, they frequently buy suits.

7. Display your chest with shirts open at the throat and partially unbuttoned. According to Molloy, women find polo shirts, in particular, to be sexy.

8. Don't wear Bermuda or walking shorts. Again, according to Molloy, women prefer shorts of shorter length.

9. Shine your shoes.

10. Don't be too proud to ask for help. Better to embarrass yourself with a friend or relative than an attractive woman you hope to impress.

## A FINAL NOTE FOR BOTH MEN AND WOMEN

You may feel uncomfortable having to alter your physical appearance in order to be attractive to the opposite sex: "If they don't like me as I am, then they can find someone else!" Unfortunately, that is exactly what is going to happen. Attractive people will be turned off to you and you'll lose out. People are unlikely to discover your inner beauty if they find your exterior to be unattractive.

# SEX AND THE SINGLE PERSON

Sex is the magnet that draws singles together for loving relationships. It's crucial, however, to know how to use its force properly so your needs are met. Unfortunately, misinformation can get in the way of healthy sexual relationships. Earlier we looked at the Myth of the Quick Shooter and the Myth of Female Frigidity. Other prevalent myths follow.

## IF I DON'T GO TO BED WITH HIM, HE'LL DROP ME
A crucial choice that most singles face is whether or not to engage in casual sex. The invention of the birth control pill in the fifties revolutionized attitudes towards casual sex so that today it's the rule rather than the exception. Simenauer & Carroll discovered that two-thirds of single men and half of single women go to bed within the first three dates. Women often feel pressured to engage in casual sex. They fear that if they don't give in to a man's sexual request in the first few dates, he will drop her. Simenauer & Carroll's survey suggests the opposite: three-quarters of the men were either against sex on the first date or at least neutral on the subject. Only one-fifth believed in the value of one night stands. It isn't surprising that only 6% of single women recommended these casual encounters. The survey suggests that millions of us are engaging in casual sex despite the fact that we really don't value it. Certainly there are many men who expect sexual intimacy early in the relationship, but there are also many who are uncomfortable with

immediate sex but feel obliged to make a pass anyway. They may actually feel relieved if they are turned down. Why then do they try to seduce women?

Ben is a 32 year old architect. "When I was younger, I automatically put the make on every girl I dated, regardless of whether or not I was attracted to her. That's the way all my friends were, too. You always tried to score, even if you were too tired or drunk to enjoy it. Now, even though I'm older and wiser, I still have that compulsion to seduce every woman I date."

Lloyd is a 44 year old school teacher. "A couple of times ladies have actually gotten angry at me for not making a pass at them. They felt insulted."

Joe is a 39 year old civil servant. "My ex-wife told me that the first time we dated she thought I was either gay or lacked self-confidence with women because I didn't try to make it with her. She laughed when I told her the reason I didn't try to ball her: I thought she was the prudish type."

First dates can be a comedy of errors where each person sacrifices to please the other. A good rule is to do what feels comfortable to you and trust the other person to do likewise. If you are a woman, never allow a man to pressure you into casual sex. If you are a man, don't feel that you have to conform to the stereotype of the makeout artist in order to be a "real man". As mentioned earlier, many men avoid sex on a casual basis. For example, Henry is a 21 year old grocery checker: "I don't feel comfortable sleeping with strangers. I know it sounds corny, but I want to get to know a woman first." Tex is a 45 year old forklift operator. "I don't like women who expect me to hop into bed with them the first time. I'm usually impotent unless I know a woman well."

## IF I GO TO BED, HE'LL THINK I'M CHEAP

Many men do look down on a woman if she is an easy conquest. Most men, however, feel differently, particularly those under 40. The vast majority no longer insist that their future wives be virgins. As a matter of fact, many men actually prefer a woman with experience.

It is difficult to predict how a man will react to you if you are a woman who has sex with him early in a relationship. In some cases, it will cause him to like you more. In

173

others, he will drop you because he has contempt for women who "sleep around". As with the previous myth, the best course is to do what feels comfortable to you.

## WOMEN SHOULD NEVER INITIATE SEX

Despite women's liberation, most feel uncomfortable initiating sex. They feel it is a man's place to make the first move. Many women fear that if they initiate sex, the man will be offended or scared off. Simenauer & Carroll's survey says the opposite: over three-quarters of men feel it is all right for women to initiate sex.

## SEX SHOULD BE SPONTANEOUS

One of the legacies of the human potential movement is an obsession with spontaneity. We are supposed to "be here now" and do whatever pops into our minds. Applied to sex this concept means that we should engage in sexual activity on the "spur of the moment" rather than plan things out carefully in advance.

Certainly there is some value to this concept. Planning, analyzing and postponing can put a damper on a sexual relationship. There are many legitimate reasons, however, for avoiding spontaneous sex:

1.  Fear of pregnancy. It's better to postpone sex than risk having an unwanted baby.

2.  Fear of discomfort. Making love on pine needles is something only masochists enjoy. Ditto for love in a volkswagen or in very cold environments. There is nothing wrong with planning ahead so that sex takes place in warm, comfortable surroundings.

3.  Fear of discovery. Sex in the outdoors or where there is little privacy may be exciting to exhibitionistic couples, but most people appreciate privacy and often need to plan for it.

Another deterrent to sexual spontaneity is the constraint of time. Better to postpone sex than to have to suffer the frustration of cutting short the act of intercourse. Also, being late to school, work or other commitment may not be worth it. As in so many other cases, it is important to avoid taking a good thing to an extreme. Spontaneous sex is to be valued only so long as it isn't stupid sex.

## SEX IS FOR THE YOUNG

There is no evidence to support this myth. Why should the joys of sex be limited to the young? The elderly are quite capable of experiencing sexual pleasure. Unfortunately, sex among the aged is frequently regarded as being deviant, sick or comical. The elderly (and even the middle-aged) often give up sex altogether because they have swallowed this myth, which is part of the American obsession with youth. "Youth is wasted on the young" and "If I only knew then what I know now" are phrases used repeatedly by mature people. They have been brainwashed into believing that life has passed them by and that certain pleasures are no longer possible or appropriate for them.

## THE PRIMARY PURPOSE OF SEX IS . . .

There are three main variations of this myth: The primary purpose of sex is 1) procreation; 2) expression of love; 3) pleasure. All of them are false. The primary purpose of sex is whatever purpose you choose to assign to it. If you desire children, the primary purpose for you may indeed be procreation. Others have no tolerance for parenthood and may prefer to engage in sex to develop intimacy in their relationships or purely for the fun of it. Beware of those who attempt to tell you what the purpose of any of your actions should be. You are your own boss and need not submit to the values of others.

## SEX IS THE MOST IMPORTANT THING IN A MARRIAGE

Many married people in this country love each other dearly and yet seldom engage in sex. To them affection, security, companionship, economics, or parenthood may be much more important than sex.

## SEX IS UNIMPORTANT IN A ROMANTIC RELATIONSHIP

This is the converse of the previous myth. In reality, sex is frequently a major cause of the downfall of romantic relationships. Surveys consistently reveal that a poor sex life is a major complaint in troubled relationships. There is

175

as great a danger of underestimating the importance of sex as there is of overestimating it.

## ALL THE GOOD MEN/WOMEN ARE TAKEN

You will be relieved to learn that this also is a myth. Many wonderful people have delayed marriage or remarriage because of other priorities: education, business, travel, personal growth or just because they haven't met the right person. The healthier, happier and more self-sufficient people are, the more likely they are to hold out for a special person. So don't conclude that single people are all losers.

## WOMEN WANT TO BE RAPED

This myth is partially based on fact. Surveys have revealed that most women have pleasurable rape fantasies. It is important to understand, however, that there is a big difference between a fantasy rape, where a woman is in complete control and can turn the fantasy off at any moment, and a real rape, where a woman often fears for her life.

A real rape can involve a great deal of physical pain as well as the dangers of pregnancy and venereal disease. Also, the men in rape fantasies are usually very attractive to the women, whereas real rapists rarely meet their victim's concept of an ideal sexual partner. So, don't confuse women's fantasies with reality. Women do *not* want to be raped.

A variation of this myth is that women who dress sexy are asking for rape. Experts tell us that physical attractiveness is usually unimportant to rapists. A homely woman is as likely to be raped as a bombshell. Clothing styles are also irrelevant. Rape is primarily an act of violence rather than sexual desire. Women who dress in a sexy or flashy manner are probably hoping to attract male attention, but this is a far cry from desiring a painful, violent experience such as rape.

## MEN HAVE IT MADE

Many women complain that society gives them a raw deal. Men have permission to try to seduce anyone who attracts them, but women are considered cheap if they do likewise. This is often true, but the other side of the coin is that being a man has major disadvantages:

176

1. He often has to put a great deal of time and effort into pursuing women.
2. He frequently spends a good deal of money on women.
3. He risks the pain of rejection.
4. He misses out on the ego boost of having women pursue him.
5. He often doesn't meet women who are secretly attracted to him.

## WOMEN HAVE IT MADE
Like the previous myth, this is only a half truth. It's often true that women only have to sit back and wait for men to do all the work. There are several disadvantages to being a woman, however.

1. She usually doesn't get to meet attractive men if they don't approach her.
2. She often doesn't feel in control. She feels forced into passively waiting for sexual partners to choose her.
3. She has to fight off obnoxious men who won't take no for an answer.
4. She is in danger of rape.
5. She is more likely to feel uncomfortable going out alone to movies, live entertainment, restaurants, parks, etc. She often winds up being bored at home.

The grass may look greener on the other side but in reality being a man or a woman has liabilities as well as benefits. The ideal solution is for men and women to take equal responsibility for initiating conversations, sexual contact, etc. They can then have the best of both worlds.

## THE PURPOSE OF SEX IS TO ACHIEVE ORGASM
Orgasm is possibly the most overestimated pleasure in our society. Due to its brevity, orgasm may give much less pleasure than kissing, hugging, etc. Many people postpone climax so as to prolong the sex act. That way they don't miss out on a non-orgasmic pleasure.

The American obsession with orgasm is derived from our emphasis on success, performance, and achieving goals rather than enjoying what we are doing. How ludicrous it is to feel frustrated and a failure because you didn't have an orgasm – "all I has was a wonderful time."

## I AM RESPONSIBLE FOR MY LOVERS' ORGASMS
You may feel an obligation to be an accomplished lover. Your ultimate fear may be to fail to bring your lover to climax. This sense of responsibility is sad for several reasons:

1.  It's hard enough to take responsibility for yourself, much less for someone else.

2.  Many women and some men have great difficulty in achieving orgasm, regardless of the proficiency of their lovers.

3.  Your sense of obligation to bring your lovers to climax is frequently contagious and leads to their sense of duty to have an orgasm to please you. Two people working to please each other may be so distracted from their own pleasure that they fail to enjoy themselves.

For too many, sex has become a job where performance is constantly evaluated. Ironically, the best sexual performers are those who are not preoccupied with being good lovers but who are free, natural and uninhibited.

## IMPOTENCE
The inability to achieve or maintain an erection can be humiliating. Several myths associated with impotence cause this needless sense of shame.

1.  *You can't be impotent if you're turned on to your lover.* Certainly a lack of sexual interest can lead to impotence. There are many other causes, however. Booze is a frequent culprit. As in the case of driving, sex and alcohol do not mix. Ironically, many men drink in order to feel more comfortable and confident with women and wind up feeling demoralized instead because of impotence. An even greater irony is the man who seduces a woman with booze, only to find that he is too drunk to take advantage of her.

178

Another cause of impotence is fear of failure. Men who feel inadequate as lovers or have had a few disastrous experiences of impotence will often feel overly tense during sex and find themselves unable to perform. Fatigue, stress and drugs are other major causes of impotence.

2.  *Occasional impotence is indicative of sexual inadequacy.* Actually, occasional impotence is experienced by most men and is no cause for alarm. As stated above, there are many circumstances that can cause impotence in men who ordinarily are quite adequate in the bedroom.

3.  *A man can overcome impotence by concentration.* In reality, concentrating on getting an erection is a sure-fire way of remaining flaccid. The more pressure you put on yourself and the more self-conscious you feel, the more difficult things become. Relaxing and thinking of other things (particularly sexual fantasies) are far more effective ways of overcoming impotence.

## WHAT DO I DO IF I'M FREQUENTLY IMPOTENT?
1.  Avoid alcohol and drugs.
2.  Avoid sex when you are tired.
3.  Avoid sex with women you find unattractive.
4.  Avoid sex when you're not in the mood. Tell her you have a headache.
5.  Learn to relax. Reread the section on relaxation in the chapter on Rejection. Also redo the exercise on page 65, substituting the fear of impotence for the fear of rejection.
6.  If you follow all of the preceding steps and continue to be frequently impotent, see a physician to determine if there is a physiological cause.
7.  If there is no physiological problem, see either a psychotherapist, sex therapist or sex surrogate. Your physician can refer you.

## WHAT DO I DO IF MY LOVER IS FREQUENTLY IMPOTENT?
1.  Encourage him to follow all seven of the steps above, if

necessary.

2. Don't ever pressure him to achieve an erection. If he could, he would.

3. Never ridicule, laugh or express anger towards him when he is impotent.

4. Help him achieve an erection through sexy attire, massage, manual or oral stimulation of the genitals, etc.

5. Let him know that there are ways for him to give you sexual pleasure other than intercourse.

## YOUR EROGENOUS ZONES

We are all individuals, so it shouldn't be surprising that we don't all enjoy stimulation of the same areas. Many women, for example, do not enjoy having their nipples or clitoris stimulated; they are too sensitive. Some men adore having their nipples stimulated; others are totally oblivious to it. Someone blowing in your ear may give you goose pimples; on the other hand, you may find that to be silly or weird.

Find out where your erogenous zones are and don't be afraid to communicate this information to your lover. Encourage your partner(s) to reveal their favorite zones as well.

## SEDUCTION

Seduction is a dirty word in many circles but in its best sense, it involves persuading someone to want to meet your romantic needs. Men (and women) who are adept at seduction don't need to be pushy or obnoxious. They know how to stimulate their would-be partners. Tyrone's advice below is for men, but can also be employeed by women.

"The secret of seducing a woman is to take an interest in her personality. Most single women are accustomed to men lusting after their bodies. This is fine but what also turns them on is your being interested in other things as well. If you convey the impression that you only find her attractive physically, you'll turn her off."

Some other keys to seduction are:

1. Be romantic.

2. Look good.

3. Be low-key and soft-sell. If you apply too much pressure or are too eager, you are likely to scare the person off.

4. Take your time. The longer you are with people, the more comfortable and secure they will feel. They will also have time to discover how attractive you are.

5. Take no for an answer graciously. "No" today may change to "yes" tomorrow. People will like you more if you respect their wishes and values. Someone really attractive should be worth the wait.

6. Make sure that their body language is positive before making your move. Check to see if they:
   • have their arms and legs uncrossed
   • are leaning towards you
   • are maintaining eye contact
   • are frequently smiling at you
   • are sitting close to you

7. Make sure their verbal behavior is also positive. If they are saying positive things and are listening closely to what you're saying, the prospects are good for seduction.

8. Find out about your competition. If you're with someone who is married, engaged or going steady, your chances are not good.

9. Find out about their availability. If they have to leave soon or feel tired, the timing may be wrong for sex.

10. Notice if they're physically aroused. The obvious sign in a man is an erect penis; in a woman, erect nipples.

11. Make sure the situation is favorable for sex. If there is little privacy or comfort, a postponement may be advisable.

12. Be aware that asking for permission often is less effective than just assuming that the answer is yes. Many

women have a policy that "if a guy has to ask, the answer is no."

13.   Gradually escalate physical contact. Light touching, light kissing and finally heavy touching is usually the most successful procedure.

## SEXUAL MORALITY

Carlene is a 34 year old supervisor for the telephone company. "I was raised in a very conservative, religious family where sex was never mentioned in polite conversation. Over the years I have tried to live up to what the Bible teaches, but it's been tough. I have strong sexual needs and occasionally break down and do things I later regret. It's hard being single and chaste."

Millions of singles find themselves in a similar predicament: their body says yes and their conscience says no. How is this dilemma to be resolved? It's not that hard to limit yourself to sex within marriage if at an early age you met someone special, got married and lived in sexual bliss ever after. What if you're single a good part or even all of your life? It's difficult to abstain from sex for long periods of time and still feel happy.

One solution is to drop all of your moral standards and engage in sex whenever you feel aroused. This course often leads to guilt and low self-esteem, however. Too many singles find themselves moving back and forth between frustration and guilt. The way to avoid both extremes is to choose one of two courses: 1) stick by your principles, or 2) change your moral views so you can live with them. A moral code that is constantly violated serves no constructive purpose. If you find yourself unwilling or unable to live by certain standards, the time has come to re-examine your sexual values.

## EXERCISE

Check all the statements that are true for you. I feel guilty if I engage in:
_____  1. an occasional one night stand
_____  2. frequent one night stands
_____  3. infrequent sex with the same person
_____  4. frequent sex with the same person

_____ 5. sex with a stranger
_____ 6. sex with a casual friend
_____ 7. sex with a good friend
_____ 8. sex with someone I love
_____ 9. sex with someone with whom I'm engaged
_____ 10. sex with someone married to someone else
_____ 11. sex with another single person
_____ 12. sex with someone of the same sex
_____ 13. sex where I seduce someone
_____ 14. sex where I lie to the other person
_____ 15. sex where I'm honest with the other person
_____ 16. sex where only I get my needs met
_____ 17. sex where both of us get our needs met.

Notice the wide variety of sexual options. If you marked some, but not all, of the statements, there is a possibility of getting your needs met and not feeling guilty. Try to limit your sexual activity to those situations where you can "have your cake and eat it too"; that is, where you can have sex and still feel good about yourself.

If you find that this is too limiting (or if you checked all the statements and, therefore, have no way of feeling good about sex as a single), consider the option of changing your sexual values. The first step is to discover how you got these values.

**EXERCISE**
1. Do the previous exercise, pretending you are your mother.
2. Do the same, pretending you are your father.
3. Do the same for any other person who has had a significant influence on your moral thinking.

It should be evident, after completing this exercise, that you have inherited your sexual values from others. How does it feel to have others running your sex life? Perhaps the time has come to develop your own moral code. Remember that the experts disagree among themselves concerning the morality of various sexual actions. Some moral philosophers condemn all forms of sexual activity outside of marriage, while others condone anything done by consenting adults. If the experts can't agree, why not make up your own mind and develop an ethical code that feels comfortable to you?

Prepare a list of sexual actions that you believe are both good for you and your partner(s). Don't allow the opinions of others or society to sway you. Make up your own mind. Once you have this list, you need to internalize your new moral code so you can act accordingly without feeling guilty. One way to do this is to visualize yourself engaging in these "approved" sexual activities.

**EXERCISE**
1.  Close your eyes and relax. Take a few deep breaths.

2.  When you feel relaxed, fantasize having sex under each of the conditions on your list of approved sexual activities. Visualize yourself the next morning after sex. How do you feel? Do you feel happy and satisfied or do you feel miserable and guilty? If you feel guilty, you still have your old moral code. Ask yourself, who am I hurting by engaging in this sexual act? Myself? My partner? If the answer is neither, you are feeling guilty purely because of values you have inherited from others. You are allowing their beliefs to cause you to violate your own needs and those of others.

Changing your moral code is never easy. It may take years before you are able to declare your moral independence. Just remember that regardless of what others tell you, your body is *yours*. You are free to do whatever you wish.

**CASUAL SEX AND INTIMACY**
One consideration in deciding whether or not it is good to engage in casual sex is whether or not it enhances intimacy. There are many people on both sides of the fence on this issue. The following comments are typical.

George is a 46 year old cartoonist. "Like most guys, I used to relish the idea of sex on the first date. One day I noticed how sex affected my casual relationships: it quickly carried them to a more intimate plane than felt comfortable to me. I reexamined my past steady relationships and realized that they all began with limited sexual contact and then gradually bloomed into heavy-duty romances. Now I resist the impulse to hop into bed the first night. The exception is if I'm with someone I'm sure I don't want to get involved with seriously. Then I have nothing to lose by having casual sex."

Marshall is a 29 year old musician. "I'm not the type to open up with a woman until after we've had sex. I find that I'm frightened of being naked emotionally, but not physically. Sexual contact opens me up and enables me to share my feelings with women."

Examine your own past relationships to determine whether casual sex enhances or prevents intimacy.

## HERPES

Another consideration with casual sex is disease. Every time you kiss or have intercourse with someone you increase the chances of being exposed to communicable illnesses. Some, like hepatitis, can be deadly. Others, like the common cold, are irritating but go away. Possibly the most dreaded disease transmitted through sexual contact is herpes. In a cover story (August 2, 1982) *Time* magazine referred to herpes as the new scarlet letter. Many people who get herpes act as if they have leprosy and are unclean. They feel obligated to isolate themselves from any sexual contact for fear of infecting others.

Horror stories such as those in *Time* have helped to create a nationwide hysteria. Three common myths about herpes have arisen:

1. *Herpes is a rare, horrible disease.* The truth is that herpes is simply a virus. The overwhelming majority of us catch herpes, just as most of us are infected by flu and cold viruses. Seventy-five percent of Americans catch chicken-pox, which is a form of herpes. Most of us also get cold sores on our lips or mouth, which are also caused by a herpes virus. Mononucleosis (more commonly known as the "kissing disease") is also a type of herpes.

   Genital herpes (herpes simplex II) causes sores on the genitals which can be quite painful. Up to 20 million Americans are estimated to have suffered from genital herpes, with a half million new cases occurring each year.

2.  *Once you get herpes, it always reoccurs.* It's true that herpes germs stay with you all of your life but this doesn't mean that you will constantly experience symptoms. Very few people experience a recurrence of the chicken-pox, for example. According to Paulette Liebman in *Whole Life Times* (July — August, 1982), one-third of those who catch genital herpes suffer only one attack. The remaining two-thirds "have recurring attacks once a year to once a month."

3.  *Only the sexually promiscuous get genital herpes.* This simply isn't true. Many people get herpes who never have sex with anyone other than a spouse or steady lover. Since most lovers are unfaithful at least some of the time, chastity may be the only effective method for avoiding infection. Even this is in doubt, since there even is some evidence that herpes can be caught without sexual contact.

    While herpes is certainly a health hazard that should not be ignored, it isn't the end of the world. It can be a severe problem for pregnant women, since the fetus is likely to die from herpes infection unless there is Cesarean delivery. For the rest of us, herpes is one of many viruses we risk catching when we associate with others, particularly on an intimate level. The solution is to become a hermit. Otherwise, go out and meet people and take your chances.

**WHAT DO I DO IF I CATCH HERPES?**

As with any illness, there are two things you should do. The first is to get it treated medically. While there is no cure for herpes, your physician or pharmacist can suggest medications that can reduce the discomfort and shorten the duration of symptoms. The second thing to do is avoid infecting others. Should you tell prospective lovers/spouses that you have had genital herpes? This is a difficult moral dilemma, since there is a small danger of infecting them even if you're careful and only have sex when you aren't experiencing symptoms. Unfortunately, because of the exaggerated fear of herpes in this country, being open about previous infection will greatly diminish your chances of making good romantic contact. How do others deal with this question?

Robert is a 38 year old bricklayer. "I found that telling women about my past experience with herpes was the kiss of death. They never wanted to have anything to do with me afterwards. Now I just keep quiet about it. If I ever get deeply involved with a lady, I'll tell her about the herpes."

Caroline is a 31 year old bartender. "I made the mistake of not telling my boyfriend that I had had herpes. I avoided sexual intercourse with him whenever I had symptoms but one time I noticed too late and he wound up catching it. He dumped me and claimed it wasn't because of the herpes but because I hadn't been honest with him."

Sarge is a 66 year old retired master sergeant. "I never tell a girl I've had herpes unless we get serious. Then I tell her because I just don't feel comfortable keeping secrets from someone I care for."

Laura is 20 years old and seeking employment. "I don't have the nerve to tell anyone I've had herpes. I keep my mouth shut and hope nobody ever catches it from me."

Noreen is a 42 year old employment counselor. "I only tell men if I've dated them for a while. I figure that if a guy dumps me because of herpes then he must not really care that much for me, so good riddance. I don't tell a guy the first few times I date him, however. That's just plain suicide."

Sanford is a 54 year old college professor. "I told a lady at a singles club about my past herpes problem. Not only did she stop seeing me but she also blabbed to her friends. Once the word was out, nobody in the club would date me. Maybe it's just my imagination, but some people even seemed to shy away from sitting next to me."

## OTHER VENEREAL DISEASES

Herpes has taken the headlines away from syphilis and gonorrhea, but these two diseases are still widespread throughout the nation. Unlike herpes, these are dangerous illnesses that must be treated. Fortunately, again unlike herpes, there are cures. See your physician or go to a special, low-cost VD clinic if one is in your area.

Next to chastity, use of a condom is the most effective way to prevent venereal disease. It is very effective with syphilis and gonorrhea but only partially so with herpes.

## INFIDELITY

More romantic relationships have foundered over the rock of infidelity than possibly any other cause. Why do most of us demand that our lovers be faithful? Sue Ann is a 44 year old travel agent. "I don't know why it's so important to me. I guess part of it is my insecurity. Dave is a charming guy and I know there are a lot of single women out there. I don't think I could bear losing him so I have a tendency to make a fool of myself when I see him talking to other women."

Roland is a 24 year old factory worker. "I take pride in the fact that I was Ruth's first and only lover. I hope I never catch some guy in bed with her because I'd probably blow him away."

Regardless of the reasons, infidelity puts a great strain on most romantic relationships. Ideally we would all be faithful to one another. Unfortunately, most people find that even if they are in love, they still are sexually attracted to others. Marital vows or commitments don't change human nature. We tend to be promiscuous in our fantasies, if not in reality. Many of us simply are unwilling or unable to be faithful to one person. The Kinsey Report back in the 1920s revealed that 80% of men and 30% of women were unfaithful to their spouses. More recent surveys by *Redbook* and *Cosmopolitan* magazines suggest that 50% or more of women practice infidelity at some time during their marriages.

One way of dealing with the question of infidelity is to have an agreement with your lover that it's okay to be unfaithful. If you don't promise to be faithful, theoretically there is no cause for resentment over other lovers. There are many different types of agreements that can work:

1. Both of you have total freedom.
2. If you take another lover, you must admit it and give your partner the same option.
3. If either of you takes a lover, it must be purely a physical relationship.
4. Either of you may take a lover but must keep it secret so the other person isn't hurt.

188

Alex is a 58 year old grocer. "Lorraine and I have an agreement not to tell if one of us takes a lover. I don't know if she's ever stepped out on me. If she does, I hope I never find out because it would really hurt. I have had two secret affairs. Lorraine never did find out and I had a ball. My affairs were a very positive experience for me and even Lorraine benefited indirectly. I became more turned on to her and to life and was a better lover and companion because of that."

Another option is to promise fidelity but cheat discreetly. This is based on the premise that "what they don't know can't hurt them." There are several drawbacks, however, to infidelity on the sly:

1.  The possibility of discovery. Laura is a 31 year old maid. "I was very careful about my extra-marital love affairs. Paul was always at the office so I was free to play around at home. Unfortunately, one day he came home to surprise me. He sure succeeded. He couldn't handle finding me in bed with another man and divorced me."

    Doris is a 39 year old saleswoman. "I was sure I never would be discovered. Otherwise I never would have risked my relationship with Steve. I took every precaution: I only cheated when I was out of town and that was with one man only. He claimed that he wasn't sleeping with anyone else but me. I wound up catching herpes from him and having to explain to my boyfriend why *he* caught it. We're still going together but I don't know if Steve has totally forgiven me."

2.  The fear of discovery. Even if you successfully conceal your romantic escapades, you may find yourself living in fear that someday you will slip or the unexpected will lead to discovery. Gail is a 26 year old secretary. "I developed an ulcer from all the worry that Jack might find out I was unfaithful to him."

3.  The problem of guilt. This is a very destructive emotion. It can wreak havoc on your self-esteem and emotional health. Tony is a 56 year old corporation executive. "I always intended to be faithful to Annie but

189

my secretary's passes were just too tempting. I wound up paying for my illicit pleasures—with guilt. I had to break off my affair because I just couldn't live with myself."

4.    The loss of intimacy. Joe is a 41 year old salesman. "Mary and I had the perfect relationship. We were as open and honest as could be. I never met anyone before that I could trust with all of my deepest secrets. On a business trip, I slept with a customer. When I got back home, I wanted to tell Mary but I just couldn't. I was afraid that she might dump me. That was unthinkable. For the first time I kept a secret from her. We're still close but now some of the magic is gone. There's an unacknowledged barrier between us that didn't exist before."

## DEVIANT FANTASIES

You probably have sexual fantasies that deviate from the norm. How you react to them has an immense effect on your psychological health. If you fail to accept your sexual thoughts and desires as a natural part of being human, you may do irreparable damage to your self-esteem. You will also cripple your capacity for healthy sexual relationships.

Repressing your sexual impulses doesn't destroy them. It only drives them underground where they fester. Trying to avoid "sick" desires and "perversions" gives them an exaggerated importance and sometimes an emotional stranglehold over your sexuality.

As an example, millions of men and women are unable to deal with their homosexual fantasies. It's common to repress any attraction to your own sex for fear of being a "faggot" or "dyke". The irony is that many experts believe that no one is exclusively heterosexual—that to some extent we are all attracted to our own sex. Dr. Albert Ellis uses a Robinson Crusoe analogy where you are alone on a desert island with someone of your own sex. Ellis claims that there would have to be something wrong with you if you *didn't* indulge in homosexuality. Regardless of whether or not this is true, the fact is that homosexual desires (and actions) are quite prevalent among supposed heterosexuals. The Kinsey Report revealed that 38% of the adult male population of the United States had engaged in at least one homosexual act "to the point of orgasm."

The tragedy is that we are taught to be ashamed of feelings and fantasies that deviate from society's mores. Ideally, we should be able to experience any feeling without guilt, shame or criticism. Our penal system punishes people for their actions rather than their thoughts and desires. If all of us who have fantasized about murder, rape or robbery were incarcerated, there might not be any jailers left to supervise the criminals. What should you do if you have uncomfortable desires?

1.   Stop trying to run away from them. To paraphrase Joe Louis, you can run away from yourself, but you can't hide.

2.   Realize that as crazy, bizarre, or abnormal as your fantasies may seem to be, there probably are millions of otherwise "healthy" people who have very similar experiences. The reason you feel alone is because most people, like you, don't broadcast to the world their deviations.

3.   Remember that you're in control and don't necessarily have to act on any of your fantasies. If you feel that you are in danger of losing control and doing something you will regret, locate a therapist to help you.

4.   Keep in mind that there are millions of happy, well-adjusted "normal" people who have sexual lifestyles that violate social conventions. Be an individual and follow the dictates of your conscience.

## TOWARDS BEING A GOOD LOVER

Being a good lover is difficult in a society that imposes so many rules and expectations upon sex. It may be valuable for you to keep the following suggestions in mind:

1.   Sex is supposed to be fun, not a job. If you are overly serious about your lovemaking, you have the wrong attitude.

191

2.   Learn to relax and let things happen. Every sexual experience doesn't have to be a "success". Some sex is good and some is bad. If you have heavy expectations, you will probably be too uptight to let go and really enjoy yourself.

3.   Take it slow. Sex is something to be savored, not rushed.

4.   Be open to experimentation. There are many ways to make love other than the "missionary position" under the covers with the lights out. You don't have to memorize the *Kama Sutra* or master hundreds of acrobatic positions. Just remember that "variety is the spice of life." Most couples have boring sex lives, which is a major contributor to the nation's high divorce rate. Boredom comes from routine, so be adventurous in your loveplay.

# WHEN LOVE DIES

Sexual attraction can cause us to fall head-over-heels in love. Temporarily it can compensate for important needs that go unmet. At some point, however, the fire of sexual attraction diminishes. The relationship then must move from a falling in love stage to what Erich Fromm calls "standing in love." This is a deeper but less-consuming love based on intimacy. The following obstacles must be faced and overcome if the relationship is to endure.

## EIGHT RELATIONSHIP KILLERS

1. Non-acceptance. All of us have the right to be ourselves and not have to live up to the expectations of others. If you pressure your partner to change into someone else, the result is usually hostility and resistance. Eventually your nagging becomes unbearable and love vanishes.

2. Concealing negative feelings. Hostility, frustration, jealousy, are frequently withheld in relationships. Holding back these negative feelings results in the loss of positive feelings as well.

3. Lack of listening. Expressing your own feelings is not enough—you must also be open to what your partner has to say. Otherwise your lover's feelings remain unknown to you until they explode.

4.  Complacency. This is taking your partner for granted ("he/she can't do without me" or "who'd marry her/him but me?") There are numerous tragic stories about partners who did find someone else despite long years invested in a marriage. Even if your lover doesn't literally leave you, taking him or her for granted can result in an emotional divorce. The relationship remains in form but not substance.

    If you find yourself feeling complacent about a relationship, ask yourself how you would feel if you lost your partner. If the grass looks greener on the other side, talk to your single friends to remind yourself about loneliness and the difficulty of finding the right person.

    Don't assume that everything is going fine in your relationship just because your partner appears happy and doesn't make any serious complaints. Your lover may be concealing all kinds of feelings. Your job is to find out where your partner is at emotionally. Presuming that he or she is satisfied is a disastrous error and can lead to your finding yourself suddenly single again. Pretend every once in a while that you're wooing your partner all over again. Make sure that important needs are not going unmet.

5.  Disrespect. There is an old saying that familiarity breeds contempt. We have a tendency to treat strangers with more respect than our loved ones. Make it the other way around. Your romantic partner is the most important person in your life and deserves your best behavior, not your worst. Intimacy is no excuse for discourtesy or cruelty. Insults or shabby treatment are not more permissible because they come from you— they hurt all the more because your actions and opinions are much more important to your loved one than those of others.

6.  Inability to compromise. While it's true that people are either compatible or they aren't, that doesn't mean that you can avoid major compromises to make a relationship work. There are some areas where it is possible to be tolerant and accepting of differences and

others where an agreement must be reached. For example:

- Child-rearing. Couples must agree on how to raise any children they may have. Even if the children are your own by a previous marriage, your new partner must have a say in how they are raised. There is no way that your loved one can be a disinterested spectator. Consistency from the adults in a home is vital. Opposing systems of discipline and reward will only lead to confusion or even in the child playing one adult off on the other. Couples must sit down and discuss, argue or negotiate a joint method of raising the children. More importantly, both of you must carry out your agreements and not revert to your own method of child-rearing.

- Lifestyle. If one of you is a jet-setter and the other a homebody, the relationship is in deep trouble. The same holds true if one person wants to live in the country and the other is a city-slicker. One or both of you will have to make significant concessions if you are to stay together.

- Money. Surveys indicate that money is the cause of more arguments among couples than anything else. Mammoth struggles have arisen over choices between a new set of golf clubs or a new jacket; a trip to Hawaii or a nest egg in the bank; hiring a maid or sending the kids off to a private school. One person in a relationship is usually more liberal about spending money than the other and a compromise must be reached.

7.  Growing apart. Invariably, people change. An ideal marriage 20 years ago may have evolved into an uneven relationship between two people with radically different values, desires, goals, talents and levels of maturity. You must either grow together or grow apart.

8.  Isolation. Frequently couples withdraw into their own

little worlds and cut off social contact with friends and relatives. Patrick is a 43 year old body and fender man. "Lola couldn't stand my mom so I had to pretty much cut off contact with my parents. She also didn't think much of my friends, so persuading her to visit my buddies or have them over for dinner was a real hassle. Lola wanted us to be an intimate twosome and was jealous of any contact I had with others, even though she knew I would never cheat on her. She just wasn't the sociable type. As the years went by, we found ourselves more and more alone. I know it sounds strange but I started to feel very lonely despite the fact that Lola was always around. I guess a lot of my needs just weren't getting met. We wound up splitting up."

There's nothing really surprising about Patrick's loneliness. No one person, no matter how wonderful, can totally fulfill you. Platonic relationships with relatives or friends are crucial to your psychological health as well as the health of your romantic relationship. Otherwise, you will place all of your needs on the shoulders of your partner, which is a crushing burden.

A certain amount of compromise is required concerning in-laws and non-mutual friends. While it's unfair for your partner to expect you to like his or her parents or friends, it is likewise ridiculous for you to demand that your partner abandon relationships with these people just because you don't like them. Your choice is to either sacrifice occasionally and put up with your partner's social circle or give your partner permission to pursue these relationships independently of you.

While you're still single, it's easy to dismiss the previous section by saying, "I'll never make those mistakes." It is guaranteed, however, that you will have to confront most if not all of the Relationship Killers in your next love relationship. Refer back to them at that time and make sure your love doesn't die needlessly.

All the books and good intentions of the world aren't enough to save a relationship sometimes. At some point you may be faced with the problem of what to do after your love dies. You may be tempted to put off a final dissolution for fear of hurting your partner. Unfortunately, procrastination rarely makes things easier. Allowing a relationship to gradually deteriorate usually leads to a great deal of bickering and resentment. Eventually you reach the point where you are so sick of the relationship that you are forced to end it immediately. The result is a nasty, unpleasant break-up. The tragedy is that you might have been able to part as friends if you had ended things when you were still on relatively good terms. While most relationships do end painfully for one or both partners, the ideal is to salvage some good and still be friends.

Dave is a 35 year old attorney. "I knew for a long time that Emily and I were going to have to split up. I know it sounds rotten, but I just got tired of her. She was a nice person but there just wasn't enough for me to stay interested. If there was something awful about her, it would have been easy to break off but I had no justification. What was I going to tell her—she was wonderful but I just didn't want to stay with her?

"Once I realized that I wanted to split up, it's amazing how things got bad so fast. We started fighting over ridiculous little things. I began to show up late for dates. I criticized Emily a lot, also. I guess I resented being stuck in the relationship and took it out on her. Anyway, things got so bad I couldn't take it. Emily was really angry when I told her I didn't want to date her anymore. I asked if we could still be friends and she laughed in my face. We work in the same office and believe me it's been hell for the last six months. I make sure to steer clear of Emily for fear of getting a withering stare."

Contrast this with the experience of Ginny, who is 34 years old and unemployed. "Don and I had a torrid romance for a few months. He had everything that turned me on in a man: looks, personality, strength. Unfortunately, the intellectual stimulation wasn't there. You can only make love so many hours and then you have to talk. I got tired of hearing about sports cars.

"Deciding to break up was tough. As I expected, Don was very hurt. He wanted to know what he could do to change and I told him nothing. I don't think there's anything bad about him—he's just not the one for me.

"It took a few months for us to start seeing each other again—on a platonic level. Now Don is one of the best friends I have. Anytime I want to go to a ballgame, I give him a call and we have a great time. I'm even friends with his new girlfriend. I'm so glad my relationship with Don didn't have to end completely."

Sometimes breaking up is not a clear-cut decision. You may have mixed feelings and not know what is best. First, you need to determine whether it's possible to salvage the relationship. While it's true that people usually won't make radical changes for you, some changes are not so difficult. Ask yourself the following three questions:

1. Have I expressed my dissatisfaction to my partner in a clear, non-threatening way? For example, saying "You're rotten" doesn't help your partner change. It's overly vague as well as insulting. Change is much more likely if you express yourself in one of the following ways:

   "I don't feel loved by you."
   "I don't feel respected by you."
   "I feel bored in this relationship."
   "My sexual needs aren't being met."
   "I feel lonely when you are away all the time."
   "I don't feel heard by you."
   "Your temper tantrums hurt me."

2. Have I made specific requests for change? Instead of asking your partner to "Be more loving" or "respect me more" or "be more exciting," have you specified exactly what you want?

   "I would like you to kiss me more often."
   "I would like you to stop interrupting me when I speak."
   "I would like us to visit other people besides your friends."
   "I would like to make love at least four times a week."
   "I would like you to cut your business travel in

half."

"I would like to have a no shouting rule."

3.    Has my partner refused to make the specific changes
      I have requested?

Unless you can answer yes to all three of these questions, you are giving up on your relationship prematurely. Give your partner the opportunity to change, even if you are pessimistic about the chances of success. If you give your partner a fair chance and nothing changes, ask yourself three more questions:

1.    Am I likely to find someone better? An appropriate
      analogy is getting rid of your used car only to buy
      another clunker that is even worse. Change is not
      always good. Anyone who says things can't get any
      worse is a fool. Things can always get worse. After
      ending a partially unsatisfactory relationship, you may
      find yourself in one far worse.
          Strangers often look more attractive than your
      partner. The reason is that you know your partner's
      faults but are probably ignorant of those of a stranger.
      All you can see is the attractive exterior of someone
      new. Make sure you don't end a semi-good relation-
      ship unless you have reasonable prospects of building
      a better one with someone else. Avoid the mistake the
      next two people made.
          Sally is a 30 year old billing clerk. "When I broke up
      with Carl, I was sure I had made the right decision.
      Carl was the John Wayne, silent type who didn't ex-
      press his feelings. I started dating guys who were the
      complete opposite and finally settled on Jerry. Every-
      thing was groovy—for a while. Then Jerry started
      flying off the handle over little things. He even threat-
      ened suicide a few times. Life with him was an emo-
      tional roller coaster. At least Carl was stable and com-
      fortable to be with. What a mistake I made letting him
      go."
          Elmer is a 43 year old stockbroker. "Doris was a
      great homemaker and mother but she didn't have
      much pizazz. After twenty years of marriage, she felt

like a comfortable old shoe. Irene, on the other hand, was sure exciting. I married her and had a ball! We were always out dancing and partying. We'd fly to Hawaii and Puerto Vallarta. Unfortunately, we started fighting over little things. When I come home, I expect food on the table and a clean house. Irene often neglected these duties, especially if she had a hangover. At other times, she would nag me because I was tired when I got home and didn't have the energy to go out and paint the town red. She was particularly sullen if I wasn't up to lovemaking. Sometimes the pressures of my job were overwhelming and I just couldn't get it up. Irene never could understand that. The worse fights were over money. I earn a good income but I can't afford the lifestyle of a sheik. Maybe I would have been better off staying with Doris. She may not have been the most exciting woman in the world but she sure was easy to get along with."

2.  Do I have the courage and strength to go it alone indefinitely? There are no guarantees that you will find a replacement right away. Are you going to have the patience to stick to your standards and wait for the right person to come along?

3.  Am I sure that I want to break up the relationship because it has gone sour, rather than because it has become too intimate? If you have been hurt in the past, you may have subconsciously resolved to never let it happen again. You may find yourself wanting to end a relationship just as it is getting good. Don't allow fear of love to ruin a wonderful relationship. A better alternative is to share your fear with your partner. You may find that this sharing makes you less afraid. Your partner will probably be supportive emotionally. You may also find that your relationship becomes far more intimate.

If you answered the last three questions affirmatively, your course is obvious: end the relationship as quickly and gently as possible.

## GETTING OUT OF A COMFORTABLE RELATIONSHIP

Joannie is a 48 year old widow. "Pete and I have broken up and gotten together again countless times. We know that there's no way we're ever going to get our needs met with each other but it sure is nice to have someone to fall back on."

Sometimes a comfortable relationship isn't beneficial. It can be an insurmountable obstacle to establishing a new relationship with someone more compatible. If you fear you are in this kind of situation, ask yourself the following question: "Do I lose the motivation to meet others because of my comfortable relationship?" Looking for someone new often requires hard work and a willingness to suffer the pain of rejection and disappointment. If you find that your motivation to meet new people is low, the likely culprit is your long-standing relationship. You may be better off severing those ties in order to free yourself for the possibility of a much more satisfying romance.

## FIFTY WAYS TO LEAVE YOUR LOVER

Paul Simon struck gold when he recorded this song. How do you end an unsatisfactory relationship? The best way, of course, is in person, unless you're physically afraid of what your partner might do. Have the courtesy to provide an explanation, but be careful not to blame your lover for the breakup or make accusations. Make "I" statements that express how unhappy you are about your needs going unmet.

How do you handle lovers who promise to reform? That depends on whether you believe them. If they have made the same promises before and failed to keep them, the logical question is "How can I be sure you mean business this time?" Unless they can come up with an awfully good answer, you would be foolish to believe them and persist in the relationship. On the other hand, if they haven't broken these specific promises, you might be wise to give them a chance. Be realistic, however. "A leopard doesn't change its spots." Don't believe people who promise to change their feelings or basic character. Only specific changes in behavior are likely.

## SURVIVING THE LOSS

While it is often very difficult to initiate a break in a

201

relationship, the real trauma comes when you suffer the misfortune of losing a loved one involuntarily. This usually creates a gaping hole in your life. You probably took for granted needs that were automatically being met by the relationship. Now they rear their ugly heads.

Losing a relationship due to death is tragic, but at least widowhood doesn't damage your self-esteem (unless you feel responsible for your partner dying). If you are dropped, however, you are likely to feel unattractive ("otherwise I wouldn't have been dumped"). Whether you are widowed, separated, or divorced, however, usually the common problem is how to mend a broken heart. You may become chronically lonely and depressed. You may constantly be obsessed about your lost lover so that you have difficulty thinking about anything else. You may despair of ever finding the right person again. Even worse is the possibility that you will be so traumatized by the experience that you never again open your heart to love. You give up on romance and become a lonely, bitter, closed person—for the rest of your life.

If you're getting over the loss of a relationship, it's common to fear that you're going insane. Be aware that a period of "craziness" is normal under these circumstances. On the average, it goes on for six months, although it certainly can continue longer. During this time, you find yourself on an emotional roller coaster of swiftly changing feelings. You may suffer from loss of sleep and appetite. You are also more likely to become physically ill since your body's resistance to disease goes down during times of stress.

Fortunately, therapists have made tremendous advances in treating this problem. Losing a relationship need not lead to interminable pain and scarring of the psyche. What can you do so you not only survive the loss but also actually bounce back as good as new?

Keeping so busy that you don't have time to experience the loss doesn't work, unless your attachment to your partner is minimal. You are running what is ultimately going to be a losing race from reality. Escaping into a new romantic relationship doesn't work either. Relationships on the rebound seldom succeed. When they end, you're back at square one: dealing with the loss of a loved one.

The first step in mending a broken heart is going

through a period of mourning. If you have been widowed, this is obvious, but the same holds true if you have been "dumped". A precious relationship has literally died. The important thing is to keep your period of mourning as short as possible so you can move on to more cheerful times. It is important to mourn properly:

1.  Go through an "orgy" of mourning. The key is to overdose during your mourning period so you rapidly get sick of it. Rather than try to avoid painful thoughts, memories, and feelings, exaggerate them. Dr. Matthew McKay, a clinical psychologist, suggests you actually "erect a shrine" to your loved one. Keep all of the sacred mementos of your relationship (articles of clothing, jewelry, awards, letters, poems, photos, etc.) in a drawer and sit and look at them for two hours each day. This may be agonizing but it's better to get it over with quickly than drag out the mourning indefinitely.

2.  Mourn on schedule, rather than when you feel like it. As human beings, we tend to rebel against anything involuntary. This is even true with mourning. If you only mourn when it feels right or convenient, you may never get sick of it. Only by forcing yourself every day to spend a designated amount of time in mourning, no matter how painful, can you become sufficiently sickened to want to end it.

3.  Focus exclusively on your lost relationship. Don't allow your mind to wander to other lost loves or problems in your life. We all have a tendency to generalize when we are depressed and think that everything in life is bad and there is no hope. You can avoid this by disciplining yourself to concentrate only on your lost relationship during your mourning time. Allow yourself to get depressed about other problems only during your "free time," that is, when you are not mourning your lost loved one.

4.  Make appointments with yourself to mourn at favorite places you visited with your loved one (restaurants,

parks, museums, sunsets, the beach, etc.).

5.  Keep busy when you're not mourning. As much as possible, limit your mourning to the designated periods and fill the rest of your time with meaningful activities. This is the antidote for depression. Unfortunately, if your depression is deep, you may not have the motivation to do anything other than wallow in your misery. If you find yourself to be almost devoid of motivation to do anything, the following suggestions may be helpful.

- Make a list of all the things you normally find enjoyable.

- Prepare a weekly schedule that includes these enjoyable activities, chores around the house and other responsibilities. For example, Murray, a 48 year old newly divorced man, prepared the following schedule:
  Monday night: visit Bill (his brother)
  Tuesday night: go out folkdancing
  Wednesday night: stay home and watch "Goldfinger" on television
  Thursday night: clean the oven and kitchen
  Friday night: go out dancing
  Saturday: do errands, play golf and then go over to Marilyn's house for dinner (Marilyn is a friend)
  Sunday: lay out in the sun and then read a Perry Mason novel that night.

- Force yourself to follow the schedule. Remember that your natural tendency is to be too lazy or depressed to do these things. Do them anyway. The secret to fighting depression is to *get moving*. What you do is less important than that you do something—anything—other than sitting home and feeling depressed.

## RECONCILIATION

The normal response to being dropped is to hope for reconciliation. If you want to leave the door open for this, try to avoid the following:

1. Screaming. Yelling at loved ones isn't going to get them back.

2. Insulting. Calling them names or accusing them of infidelity will likewise only push them farther away.

3. Begging. If the person needs to be begged to stay with you, obviously there are no prospects for a happy, healthy and stable relationship. Begging only makes you look pathetic and contemptible.

Your beloved may have a change of heart and come back, but not because of anything you do. If your former partner discovers a need for you, it's possible that a reconciliation will occur. Your attempts to encourage this, however, will only backfire.

## THE GOLDEN OPPORTUNITY
It may be trite, but every cloud can have a silver lining. If you asked the millions of happy couples in this country, they would tell you how glad they are that their previous relationships failed, despite the heartache. Being single is a golden opportunity to meet someone special. This book is aimed at helping you find that person as quickly as possible. Suppose you follow the suggestions given and still don't meet the right person. What's the problem?

1. You may be afraid of love. You may need more time to recover from a broken relationship. If years have gone by and you still aren't ready for a new love, see a psychotherapist.

2. You may have a fatal flaw: something about you that turns people off. It may be the way you dress or smell or something more subtle. If you have close friends, ask them what it might be. Put some pressure on them by letting them know how important it is for you to discover the problem, no matter how embarrassing it may be.

205

3.     You may not be working hard enough to find the right person. Redouble your efforts.

4.     On the other hand, you may be trying too hard. Don't scare people off by being too serious about making contact with them. Relax and be "cool" when you meet people. Don't think you have to hit it off with every single you meet. There is no limit to the number of attractive people. You only have to succeed with one of them.

5.     You haven't waited long enough. The person you are hoping to meet may come along tomorrow—or next year. There is such a thing as luck and maybe you haven't been blessed with it so far. Try to be patient and wait for your luck to change. In the meantime, it's crucial that you make your single lifestyle as comfortable as possible, so you don't get desperate and escape into a relationship with someone inappropriate. You need to be happily single, which is the topic of the next chapter.

# SURVIVING AS A SINGLE

Cindy is 30 years old. Her husband Bill recently died in a motorcycle accident. There was no life insurance. Since she's never worked outside her home, she's having difficulty finding employment. She spends most of her time in her studio apartment alone, since she has little money to go out and have a good time. She finds herself less welcome at her friends' homes—she's now the only single in a social circle of couples. Her friend Elizabeth has even admitted to a fear that "you may try to move in on my husband now that you're single and lonely." Cindy finds herself economically and emotionally depressed. She spends a lot of time meditating on how "unfair life is."

Mickey is a 43 year old liquor salesman. His wife divorced him because "we're no longer on the same wavelength." She got the house and the kids; Mickey got most of the bills and the burden of finding another place to live.

Cindy and Bill are discovering the liabilities of the single lifestyle. They have joined 60 million Americans who must answer two vital questions: 1) how do I survive financially as a single; and 2) how do I deal with the loneliness?

## WHERE TO LIVE

An important decision that affects both questions is whether to live alone (assuming that you don't have custody over children) or with others. There are many advantages to living alone, particularly the privacy. Before choosing this option, however, consider the two main disadvantages: the added expense and the danger of loneliness. If you should decide to live alone, three low-cost options are: living on a boat, in a mobile home, or in a studio (one-room) apartment. If you decide that it would be more advantageous to live with others, consider the following options:

1. Living with relatives (e.g., your parents, adult children, siblings).
2. Living with friends.
3. Living with strangers.

If you should decide to live with relatives or friends, ask yourself whether you are willing to risk the loss of a valuable relationship. You may discover that you can appreciate your friends or relatives in small doses but not full-time. If you should decide to live with strangers, there are several things you need to consider.

1. Do I want to live with someone of the same or opposite sex? Living with someone of the same sex is more common but many singles claim that residing platonically with someone of the opposite sex is better. Ellen is a 38 year old divorcee. "I've tried rooming with women but we wind up competing for the same guys. Living with a man is far easier. Besides, it's nice to have a man around the house."
   Don't make the mistake of assuming that it's impossible for people of the opposite sex to be platonic roommates. Millions of singles have successfully lived together without sexual interaction.

2. Do I want to live with one roommate or many? Communal households of three or more singles are not uncommon in this country. One advantage is you can afford to rent a far larger and more expensive home. Communal households even exist in mansions.

3. Do I have the personality or temperament to live harmoniously with a stranger? If you are the type who finds it difficult to tolerate bad habits, it might be better to go it alone.

4.    Where do I locate my roommate(s)? The typical way is to place or answer an ad in the classified section of your local newspaper. Other sources of ads are bulletin boards in laundromats, supermarkets, churches and college campuses. Roommate bureaus can also be an excellent way. Usually you receive kitchen privileges as well as your own bedroom. Another possibility is living in a boarding house where you receive your meals as well as lodging.

If you do decide to live with others, it's advisable to be clear before moving in concerning how the household chores will be distributed. A harmonious household of singles is possible only if everyone takes equal responsibility for making the home clean and comfortable. Otherwise there will be constant resentments and arguments. Many communal households set up rigid schedules as to when the cleaning will be done and who will perform the necessary chores.

If you have custody over children, you obviously have less freedom of action. The suggestions above are still appropriate, however. It is becoming more and more common for single parents and their children to live in communal households with similar families.

## FINANCIAL SURVIVAL

Two may not be able to live as cheaply as one, but it certainly is more economical. Men who have just split with their wives often have to support two households. The former wife doesn't have things much better. For example, Alexandra is a 39 year old former school teacher. "When I divorced Martin, I was super-confident that I would have no financial problems. I had been a school teacher for several years before my marriage and figured that I could always go back to the classroom. The only problem was that my teaching credential had expired. I would have had to go back to college and take several courses. Even if I got the credential renewed, teaching jobs are few and far between. I was stuck with Martin's alimony payments, which weren't enough to live on and continue with the mortgage payments. I lost my home and had to live like a poor person for the first time in my life."

Andy is a 42 year old businessman. "I thought that the hard part of adjusting to the divorce was going to be missing my children. It turned out that my biggest problem was poverty. I had to move from our comfortable middle class home in the suburbs to a studio apartment in the city. Vacations, golfing, expensive clothes all became luxuries that I just couldn't afford. The worst thing was having to learn how to cook, since I couldn't afford to eat out. It isn't much fun being a member of the Swanson set."

If you're newly divorced, there are several things you can do to insure that being single doesn't become economic disaster.

1. Use or develop a high-paying skill. If you have been out of the job market for a long time or have a low-paying job, it's vital to make some changes. There are a number of options you need to consider if you don't have the prerequisites for a high-paying job:

   • going back to college and completing a degree
   • going to graduate school and getting an advanced degree
   • going to a commercial school that teaches a specific skill (e.g., real estate, radio-television announcing, cosmetology, secretarial skills, data processing)
   • taking a correspondence course through the mail
   • learning a valuable skill at a community college or government retraining center.

   The crucial thing, of course, is to develop a *marketable* skill. Studying liberal arts probably won't enable you to get a high-paying job. If you're in a financial position to support yourself comfortably without learning a new skill, then by all means take courses for enjoyment or the love of learning.

   Be aware of the hazards of working full-time during the day and studying part-time at night. Millions have done it, but it's no picnic. Make sure that you have the physical and mental toughness to succeed with a work/school lifestyle.

2. Learn about money. There are numerous adult educa-

210

tion classes available at local high schools and community colleges dealing with money management and related subjects. Along with learning valuable information, you also might meet someone special.

3.    Investigate low-cost or free community services. The local legal aid society may be able to help you with your legal needs. Free medical care is often available, as well as free or low-cost psychotherapy. You may have to put some real time and effort into locating these community services, but they are there. Call your local newspaper, church, community agency or city hall for information.

4.    Avoid plastic. Credit cards can be the road to bankruptcy. Unless you are sure that your income will soon increase significantly, it makes no sense to go out and purchase expensive clothes, furniture, appliances, etc.

5.    Don't be afraid to ask for help from friends and relatives. Asking for a loan can be risky: it may put a strain on an important friendship. On the other hand, it may be better to temporarily impose on someone than live a bleak existence.

6.    Consider the possibility of joining the armed forces. The pay isn't good but at least your basic financial needs will be met. There are also extensive training programs that teach valuable skills. Veteran's benefits are also available to finance a return to school when you leave the military.

7.    Learn how to develop a budget and live by it. If your spouse always handled financial matters, you may find yourself unable to keep your income and expenditures in balance. There are numerous books that teach you how to plan a budget. You may prefer to take a course at a local school or college. If you want to teach yourself how to budget, start by listing the following:

    • long-term debts and financial obligations and when

they are due.
- monthly "automatic" expenses (e.g., rent, alimony, child support, food, clothing, auto expenses, insurance).
- discretionary expenses (e.g., entertainment, sports, socializing).
- sources of income, including wages, dividends, etc.

Hopefully your expenses will be balanced by your income. Otherwise you need to eliminate or reduce some expenses or increase your income. Remember that it's easy to plan a budget. The hard part is sticking to it, no matter how much it hurts.

After you find yourself above water financially and living comfortably, your next goal may be to achieve financial independence. Then you won't be tempted to marry in order to enhance your lifestyle.

## LONELINESS
Simenauer & Carroll report that 85% of singles complain about loneliness, making it the most common and most painful experience of singles. Unfortunately, the lonelier you are the more likely you are to become desperate and get involved with inappropriate people.

You are likely to feel most lonely under the following circumstances:

1. Holidays, particularly Thanksgiving, Christmas and New Year's Eve.
2. Friday and Saturday nights (if you don't have a date or a relationship, it can be embarrassing as well as lonely).
3. Birthdays.
4. When someone close to you dies. A sense of your own mortality can overwhelm you at such times. The result is depression and loneliness.

## STRATEGIES FOR DEALING WITH LONELINESS
1. Be prepared. Don't be surprised when loneliness strikes. For most of us it is inevitable, particularly during the periods listed above. If you realize that loneliness is coming, it won't be so traumatic.

2.  Accept it. Running away from loneliness doesn't work in the long run. Say, "this is just one of the times that I feel lonely and I'll just have to grin and bear it." As J. Krishnamurti put it, "When the pain of loneliness comes upon you, confront it, look at it without any thought of running away. If you run away, you will never understand it and it will always be there waiting for you around the corner."

**EXERCISE**

If you have trouble being alone for even short periods of time, you need to toughen yourself.

a. Schedule a specific amount of time for being alone. You may wish to start with one hour.

b. Eliminate escapes from your solitude during this period. For example, disconnect your telephone or take it off the hook. Keep your radio, television and stereo off. Spend the entire time by yourself. You may choose to read, work around the house or just sit and think.

c. Avoid eating, smoking and drinking during your period of solitude. They are also escapes from loneliness.

d. Gradually increase the amount of time you can spend in complete solitude. After a while, you hopefully will be able to increase your time alone to an entire evening. On the other hand, if you can't even tolerate one hour of solitude, start off with an even shorter period.

3.  Develop activities you can enjoy when you are alone. If you are accustomed to always having people around when you do things, you have a problem. You may need to discover the joys of solitude: dining, watching movies, walking and thinking—alone. Part of the problem may be that you are embarrassed being alone in a restaurant, theater, beach or park. Rather than be embarrassed, take pride in the courage it may take for

213

you to do these things alone. Look around and you will see others who are also alone. Many of them are probably having a better time than if they were with someone.

4.    Avoid the triggers of loneliness. Find out when you habitually become lonely and see if you can eliminate the cause. For example, Rona is a 66 year old woman. "I love romantic novels and movies. The only problem is I frequently feel very lonely afterwards. I've had to give them up in order to avoid deep depressions."

Al is a 73 year old widower. "For years after my wife died, I kept her clothes in the closet. Every time I saw them I felt so lonely. It took a lot of strength but I finally managed to take them all down to the local thrift shop. I also put all of her photographs in the attic rather than keep them prominently displayed in the house. Now I'm not constantly reminded of how beautiful she was."

Joe is a 31 year old businessman. "I have a tendency to get lonely when I drive alone. I pretty much solved the problem by joining a carpool since most of my driving is commuting back and forth to work."

Nora is a 39 year old medical aide. "I get most lonely around newlyweds. Since I play the organ, I frequently was asked to perform during weddings at the local church. I finally quit doing it and my loneliness has really gone down."

If you're not sure what triggers your loneliness, keep a diary. Each time you feel lonely, jot down the circumstances. Eventually you should discover one or more triggers and be able to eliminate them.

5.    Keep busy. The more active you are, the less you will feel down and depressed. Physical activity is particularly recommended:
- run around the block
- clean the house
- mow the lawn
- do five laps around the swimming pool
- take a shower
- go for a walk or hike

214

- fix the car
- go for a drive
- visit someone

6. Get involved in things that require a good deal of time and energy:
   - a regular exercise program
   - sports teams and leagues
   - classes
   - volunteer work

7. If you're unemployed, get a job (even if you don't need the money).

8. Share your lonely feelings with someone. Call or visit someone who cares for you. If you have no one appropriate, go out and find another single person and set up an agreement whereby either of you can call one another when lonely.

9. Build a large social network of both casual and intimate friends. Your casual friends should fill a particular need; for example, someone who enjoys fishing, golfing, or playing cards with you. Your intimate friends are those who care about you. Don't make the mistake of underestimating the value of these platonic friendships. Single people have a tendency to put so much energy into meeting people for romantic purposes that they miss out on many opportunities to form beautiful platonic friendships, particularly with members of the opposite sex. Men and women can get close without engaging in sex. To do so requires the following:
   - men must realize that they don't have to "put the make" on every woman
   - women have to realize that not every man is "hot for my bod"
   - sexual tension between platonic friends should be brought out in the open so it doesn't serve as an unacknowledged barrier between them.

Time is a crucial factor. You must take time for

your friendships if they are to thrive. No matter how busy you are, it's important to see your friends regularly rather than once in a blue moon. Otherwise they wither on the vine. For example, Sal is a 29 year old butcher. "Bill and I have been best friends for fifteen years. Even though we live within 20 miles of each other, we have a tendency to not see each other regularly. We finally had to make a rule to get together every Saturday afternoon except in special cases. The constant contact means that we stay very close and are able to get things off our chests when we are troubled and need emotional support."

Singles are often viewed by society as pitifully lonely people. Marriage is seen as an insurance policy that protects people from loneliness. Actually the loneliest of all are those who are trapped in a miserable marriage and have despaired of ever getting their needs met. As a single person, at least you have the hope of a satisfying relationship. Open yourself to those around you who are also searching for love and your hope will become a reality.

# ROMANCE

"Whatever happened to romance?" asks Lorna, an 18 year old student. "The men I meet all treat me like I'm one of the guys. They don't seem to know what flowers are for or how to make a girl feel special. If being liberated means throwing romance out the window, maybe I should have been born 50 years ago."

Rex is a 27 year old commercial fisherman. "I'd feel like a jerk bringing flowers or candy to a girl. Besides, they're really expensive nowadays."

Rolly is a 41 year old employment counselor. "I once had a lady bring me flowers. You could have knocked me over with a feather! After I recovered from the shock, I found a makeshift vase. For the next few days, I had fond thoughts of Sally each time I looked at the flowers. Now that I know how romantic they are, I always bring flowers the first time I date somebody (and other times, too)."

The vast majority of single women like romantic men. Flowers or candy definitely are not considered to be corny. The women who bring small gifts to men usually get a good reception also. Other all-time romantic favorites of both men and women are:

- candlelight
- soft music
- sunsets
- champagne
- warm, cozy fires

Thank you notes are also valued. When people spend money

on you, go out of their way to please you or are just thoughtful, it's good manners to express your gratitude at the time and also later through a note.

Romantic couples don't wait for formal dates to be in contact. They frequently telephone each other just to say hello or share some news. Love letters are also very romantic. Many men avoid such romantic gestures for fear of appearing foolish, feminine or too eager. Thoughtfulness and kindness *never* make a bad impression on either sex.

Compliments are another vital part of romance. If a woman spends a few hours trying to look extra nice, she expects you to notice and comment upon it. Don't admire her beauty silently. Let her know that you appreciate her. Likewise, if a man is well-dressed or well-groomed, he enjoys hearing you express your appreciation. If you're dating someone, there must be things about them that you find attractive. If you frequently compliment them the chances for romance increase. This doesn't mean that you should resort to flattery. If you can't sincerely compliment someone why are you in the relationship?

Frequently someone you compliment may "flick it off" by disagreeing. Don't make the mistake of concluding that the compliment was unappreciated. Unfortunately, society teaches us that to feel good about ourselves is to be conceited. Susan is a 40 year old realtor. "I've noticed that I frequently feel embarrassed when someone says something nice about me. Later in the week, though, I tend to treasure the compliment." So don't be afraid to say nice things to people.

Another key to romance is privacy. Private dinners at home can be far more romantic than meals at fancy restaurants. If you have custody over children, arrange for a relative, friend or babysitter so you can be alone with your date. This doesn't mean that you should hide your children. Family outings and dinners are fine as long as there are also times when there's just the two of you. Babysitting can be expensive but the added romance justifies it.

Vacations, from an overnight trip to an expensive cruise, can rekindle the fires of love. Experiencing each other in new places and situations can bring excitement back into a too-comfortable relationship. Don't always go to the same restaurant or theater, see the same friends, or engage in the same sports, games or hobbies. Variety is the spice of life. Lovers who don't have new experiences with you may seek them with others.

Ultimately the key to romance is communicating that you care through words and actions. The most effective way to get this message across is with three words: I love you. Unfortunately, many people shy away from saying this. Some common excuses are:

1. My lover already knows. If you're the kind of person who is very affectionate, both verbally and physically, your lover probably does know. Say it anyway. Many people are insecure and need to be reassured that you love them. Also, hearing "I love you" brings tremendous pleasure to most people. If you're not the affectionate type, you definitely need to say "I love you." That may be the only way to get the message across.

2. Saying "I love you" means I have to love you all the time. John is a 38 year old stonemason. "Whenever I try to say I love you, I almost choke on the words. I sometimes feel love for people but at other times I feel angry or even hateful towards them. Most of the time, I don't feel either loving or hating. I don't want to lie and say "I love you" unless I'm sure that it isn't just temporary. I have to be sure that I'll feel the same way tomorrow."

Many have this distorted view of love as a constant state. In reality, nobody ever loves anyone all the time. The capacity to love includes the potential for hate. The people you care for the most have the ability to hurt you deeply so it's normal to feel anger, bitterness, frustration, jealousy, disappointment, and even hatred sometimes towards your loved ones. Emotions tend to be short-term and inconsistent.

When you tell people you love them, you are telling the truth—if you love them at that moment. Tomorrow you may feel differently. What you said the day before doesn't revoke your right to feel negative emotions or even apathy towards your loved one today.

3. Love is scary. It certainly is. Most of us have exper-

ienced the pain associated with a love relationship that doesn't work out. Avoiding the words "I love you" can be a way of denying the seriousness of the relationship and, therefore, protecting you from the heartache of a breakup. Unfortunately, it can also be a very effective way of insuring the end of a relationship. A relationship where love goes unacknowledged has less chance of survival than one where the lovers are open about their feelings and willing to risk the pain of a romance that dies.

4.    My lover feels uncomfortable when I speak of love. Saying "I love you" can freak your partner out, so you may wish to play it cool. If you suspect your partner is afraid of love, you may have to be patient and hold your tongue. But don't wait too long. Better to end things than continue with someone who may never be secure enough to handle a loving relationship. As with compliments, don't hold back loving statements just because your lover is slightly uncomfortable. After the initial discomfort, your partner may cherish your statement of love.

## OTHER WAYS OF SAYING I LOVE YOU
In addition to words, there are many non-verbal ways of saying "I love you". Touching is crucial—and not just as foreplay in the bedroom. Society has many touching taboos, so it isn't easy. There are four things you can do to break down these barriers.

1.    Sit next to each other. If you're in separate chairs or at opposite ends of the room, there is little opportunity to touch one another. If you own a large car and pull down the armrest, the chances of touching decrease. The closer you are physically, the more likely you are to touch each other.

2.    Massage one another. There are numerous classes in massage available all over the country. You can learn all the fancy strokes the professionals use or skip the classes and experiment on your own. Massage can be sensual as well as sexual, so don't feel obligated to

engage in sex each time.

3.      Touch each other casually. There are numerous opportunities to do this each day. Touching doesn't always have to escalate to sexual contact.

4.      Kiss each other spontaneously. If you only give hello or goodbye kisses or limit your kissing to the bedroom, your relationship is sadly deficient in romance. There's nothing wrong with a spontaneous kiss for no reason other than your feeling affectionate.

Your actions always speak louder than words. If you cancel some activity, business meeting or other plan in order to be with your lover, you are very effectively communicating your love. Time is a wonderful gift. Turning off the radio, stereo or television; closing your newspaper, magazine or book; and dropping whatever you're doing are excellent ways of saying I love you. Spending time together is not enough—it has to be quality time. If you find that you're spending a great deal of time together physically but are off in different worlds intellectually and emotionally, your romance is either dead or dying.

Helping one another in various tasks can bring a sense of togetherness to a relationship. Helping your lover with the housework, car repair, business or school assignments can actually be romantic. Even if your "help" isn't all that helpful or needed, it's the thought that counts.

Sometimes just being with each other is all that's necessary. Romance doesn't always require conversing, touching, kissing, making love or doing things together. A quiet evening where virtually nothing happens can enhance your intimacy.

## OPTIONS

Once you feel confident you're with the right romantic partner, you have several choices. The first possibility is to remain uncommitted. There are several advantages to this:

1.      Freedom. Both of you may date other attractive people.

2.   Comfort. Some people are only able to love and enjoy someone so long as it is voluntary and not experienced as an obligation. You may feel uncomfortable being in a committed relationship.

3.   Privacy. You are able to be alone whenever you want.

4.   Fear. You may be afraid that commitment will only spoil a good relationship. There is no shortage of examples of pleasant relationships that collapsed after lovers moved in together or got married.

Another option is to date each other exclusively. This is known as going together or going steady. Ideally this is a mutual decision. What do you do if your partner is reluctant to meet your request for a committed relationship?

1.   You can offer your lover an ultimatum: "Agree to a committed relationship or lose me." This is a very poor way to cement a romantic partnership. Forcing a person into a commitment inevitably leads to resentment. Furthermore, a forced commitment isn't as reliable as a voluntary one. There is no guarantee that your lover will keep a promise to date you exclusively. The biggest disadvantage to this approach is that your romantic partner may choose to respond to your ultimatum by breaking off the relationship. You are then left with a painful void in your life.

2.   You can give your partner more time to feel more favorable towards a commitment. Ask him or her to share any fears or misgivings. Possibly you can reassure your partner. Your patience may enable your lover to eventually feel comfortable about making a commitment.

3.   You can give in to your lover's need to avoid an exclusive relationship. This is the best course *if* you can be happy in an uncommitted relationship.

4.   You can end the relationship. If you can't be happy in a non-exclusive relationship, don't want to force your

lover into an involuntary commitment, and find that patience doesn't work, this is the inescapable alternative.

Suppose the shoe is on the other foot: your lover wants a committed relationship and you don't. What do you do? Ideally you stick to your guns and refuse to make a commitment until it feels comfortable. You don't always have that luxury, however. What if your partner presents you with an ultimatum? Then you must weigh the discomfort of commitment versus the pain of losing your lover.

A committed relationship frequently leads to a choice between living together, also know as cohabitation, and marriage. Why don't people who live together just get married?

1.  They aren't sure about the permanence of their relationship. The average cohabitation period is 2 to 3 years. Many couples consider it to be a trial marriage. If they can stand living together 24 hours a day, they may be candidates for a successful marriage.

2.  They want the freedom to break up. Many singles are unwilling to make an ironclad commitment to stay together permanently, through thick and thin. Avoiding marriage theoretically means that each partner can leave without feeling guilty and suffering recriminations.

3.  They hope to avoid the legal difficulties of divorce. Divorce can be expensive and time-consuming. Cohabiting couples can break up quickly and cheaply.

4.  They don't believe in marriage. Some singles consider it to be an archaic institution which serves no useful purpose.

5.  They desire the economic advantages of cohabitation. The tax code sometimes discriminates against married couples. Elderly couples find that they get larger pensions if they cohabit rather than marry. Cohabitation can also be advantageous to you if you earn

considerably more than your partner. Unlike divorcing couples, you won't have to share property or income with your partner after a breakup.

In recent years, there has been considerable confusion due to litigation such as the Lee Marvin "palimony" case, where the actor was sued by his former live-in lover, Michelle Triola. More recently, tennis champion Billie Jean King was sued by her lesbian lover. There no longer are any guarantees that you won't have to share your fortune with former live-in lovers. Several precautions should be taken by couples living together:

1.  Make sure that you are both clear about who owns what (and who *owes* what). Don't wait until you're breaking up to decide these things. Ideally you will have a written agreement, signed by both parties, that deals with property and debts. Making such an agreement is not very romantic, but it avoids a great deal of acrimony after the breakup.

2.  If you don't have a written agreement, make sure you have proof of ownership of your personal property. If you place a home, automobile or other item in both names, your partner is legally entitled to one-half ownership, unless you have a bill of sale or other proof that you paid for it by yourself.

3.  It's wise to keep separate bank accounts and credit cards. Otherwise, you run the risk of your partner cleaning out your mutual accounts and running up debts for which you will be responsible.

Despite all the publicity for living together arrangements, matrimony is still the preferred option for most committed couples in America. If the institution of marriage is dying, as some pundits claim, it's quite a lively corpse! Why do couples choose matrimony?

1.  Social pressures. Living together often leads to disapproval from parents, friends and business associates.

2. Religious values. Cohabitation is considered to be "living in sin" by most churches.

3. Security. One or both partners usually feel insecure if there isn't a marital contract. Marriage suggests permanence. This is despite the fact that the average marriage in America only lasts seven years.

4. Children. Potential parents are worried about their child being called a bastard or "love child".

5. Economic discrimination. Promotions in corporations traditionally go to "stable" married men rather than single men or women. There is still a great deal of economic discrimination against singles or cohabiting couples. They are seen as poor risks.

6. Housing advantages. It's easier to rent or buy a home if you are married because you are viewed as being more reliable.

7. Financial security. If you take care of the home while your partner works, you are in a vulnerable position without a marriage contract. Your contribution to the home may be every bit as important and valuable as that of the breadwinner but after a breakup, you may be left with virtually no money or possessions. Marriage helps insure you will get your due financially.

8. Romantic reasons. Most singles find marriage to be far more romantic than cohabitation. They agree with the song that says, "Love and marriage go together like a horse and carriage."

Possibly the main reason for avoiding marriage is the fear of divorce. There is no way of insuring a marriage will last, but there are three precautions you can take:

1. Ask youself, "How well do I know this person?" Time is often a good test. If you have known your partner for less than a year, you may be ignorant of important information. The same is true if either of you have a

tendency to conceal feelings. Before getting married, put your cards on the table and get your intended to do the same.

2.   Also ask yourself, "Have we gotten past the honeymoon stage?" This may sound ridiculous, since you haven't even gotten married yet. As stated earlier, there is a great difference between falling in love and "standing" in love. The time to get married is *after* the bubble has burst: you have had some major arguments and problems but still want a committed relationship. Don't wait until after the wedding to have your first fight.

3.   Make sure you have discussed and reached agreement on the following:
     ● whether or not to have children and how many
     ● whether one or both of you will hold a job
     ● where you will live and how much you will spend for housing
     ● whether each of you has the right to be who you are or are expected to change.

If you disagree on any of these vital issues, you need to postpone or even terminate your plans for marriage. Otherwise, you may be condemning yourself to a lifetime of unhappiness or the trauma of divorce.

Today in America being single is finally recognized as a valid lifestyle. You may be able to find happiness without a committed relationship. Most people, however, don't feel completely satisfied unless they are in an exclusive relationship, preferably marriage. Make up your own mind. Don't feel compelled to get married just because "everyone else is". Be an individual and choose the lifestyle that makes you happiest.

# AN OPEN LETTER TO SINGLE MEN

I'm a single woman looking for the right man for a romantic relationship. It's discouraging sometimes. You can make things a lot easier for me by doing the following:

1.  Don't stay at home—I'll never be able to meet you.

2.  Make yourself available by going to places that I frequent.

3.  Don't be afraid to approach me. You're doing me a favor by breaking the ice.

4.  Give me the same privilege of initiating contact with you.

5.  Don't expect me to hop into bed just because you feel turned on. I may not feel like it. And don't think that I owe you my body just because you took me out on a date or bought me a drink.

7.  When we first meet, don't tell me I'm the most beautiful woman you've ever met or that you are madly in love with me. I'm not dumb enough to swallow that.

8.  Don't talk to me like I'm one of the guys in the locker room. I'm not.

9.  Control your drinking. Too much booze makes you very unattractive to me.

10. Please be patient and wait for me. Don't marry someone wrong for you before I have a chance to meet you.

Sincerely,

Ms. Right

227

# AN OPEN LETTER TO SINGLE WOMEN

I am a single man looking for someone special for a loving relationship. It isn't easy. You can facilitate things for me by doing the following:

1. Don't stay at home—I'll never be able to meet you.

2. Make yourself available by going to places I frequent.

3. If you're open to meeting me, let me know. A smile, eye contact, standing or sitting next to me are all ways of tipping me off that you find me attractive.

4. Take the initiative. I may be too shy to say hello, but that doesn't mean I don't want to meet you.

5. Don't expect me to be witty, charming, clever or profound in the first four minutes we talk. Give me time to relax and find something we have in common.

6. Don't judge me harshly because you've had bad experiences with other men. I am a unique person and deserve to be treated accordingly.

7. Don't be on the defensive if I approach you. I know some guys are rotten, but I'm different.

8. Don't assume that I want to go to bed with you. I might want to get to know you first.

9. Don't be a tease and pretend you want to sleep with me if you don't.

10. Don't play hard to get. I only have so much nerve and motivation. I may give up on you quickly unless you give me some encouragement.

11. Please be patient and wait for me. What a tragedy it

would be if you married the wrong person before you got a chance to meet me.

Sincerely,

Mr. Right

# SUGGESTED READING

Bach, G.R., and Deutsch, R.M. *Pairing.* NY: Avon Books, 1970.

Branden, N. *The Psychology of Romantic Love.* NY: Bantam Books, 1981.

Coleman, E., and Edwards, B. *Brief Encounters.* Garden City, NY: Anchor Books, 1979.

Collins, E. *The Whole Single Person's Catalog.* NY: Peebles Press, 1979.

Edwards, M., and Hoover, E. *The Challenge of Being Single.* NY: New American Library, Inc., 1975.

Hanson, D. *How To Pick Up A Man.* NY: G. P. Putnam's Sons, 1982.

Johnson, S.M. *First Person Singular: Living The Good Life Alone.* NY: New American Library, Inc., 1978.

Krantzler, M. *Creative Divorce.* NY: New American Library, Inc., 1975.

McKay, M., Davis, M., Fanning, P. *Thoughts & Feelings: The Art Of Cognitive Stress Intervention.* Richmond, California: New Harbinger Publications, 1981.

Molloy, J.T. *Dress For Success.* NY: Warner Books, 1975.

Simenauer, J., and Carroll, D. *Singles: The New Americans.* NY: Simon and Schuster, 1982.

Wanderer, Zev and Cabot, Tracy, *Letting Go: A Twelve Week Personal Action Program To Overcome A Broken Heart.* NY: Warner Books, 1981.

Wassmer, A. *Making Contact.* NY: The Dial Press, 1978.

Weber, E. *How To Pick Up Girls.* NY: Symphony Press, 1970.

Weiss, R.S. *Marital Separation.* NY: Basic Books, Inc., 1975.

*Richard Gosse is co-author of THE DIVORCE BOOK, New Harbinger Publications, Oakland, California, 1984.*